Richard ▇▇▇▇▇▇▇▇▇▇▇▇▇▇▇▇▇▇▇▇▇▇▇▇▇▇ He was
senior p▇▇▇▇▇ of a ▇▇▇▇▇▇ ▇▇▇ and dire▇▇or of a
number of entrepreneurial companies before becoming
one of the founders of the ▇▇▇▇▇▇▇▇▇▇▇▇▇▇▇▇▇▇

Also by Richard Murphy

TAX HAVENS: HOW GLOBALIZATION REALLY
WORKS (*with Ronen Palan and Christian Chavagneux*)

THE COURAGEOUS STATE

OVER HERE AND UNDERTAXED:
MULTINATIONALS, TAX AVOIDANCE AND YOU

For more information on Richard Murphy and his
books, see his website at www.taxresearch.org.uk

THE JOY OF TAX

How a fair tax system can create a better society

Richard Murphy

CORGI BOOKS

TRANSWORLD PUBLISHERS
61–63 Uxbridge Road, London W5 5SA
www.penguin.co.uk

Transworld is part of the Penguin Random House group of companies whose
addresses can be found at global.penguinrandomhouse.com

Penguin
Random House
UK

First published in Great Britain in 2015 by Bantam Press
an imprint of Transworld Publishers
Corgi edition published 2016

A CIP catalogue record for this book
is available from the British Library.

ISBN
9780552171618

Typeset in 11/15pt Sabon by Falcon Oast Graphic Art Ltd.
Printed and bound by Clays Ltd, Bungay, Suffolk.

Penguin Random House is committed to a sustainable
future for our business, our readers and our planet. This book is made from
Forest Stewardship Council® certified paper.

MIX
Paper from
responsible sources
FSC® C018179

1 3 5 7 9 10 8 6 4 2

To James and Thomas, their friends, and all in their generation, in the hope that this might sort out some of the mess we've made for you.

Contents

Contents

Introduction

I can't remember when Alex Cobham, now of the Tax Justice Network, joked that I should write a book called *The Joy of Tax*. I have to thank him for the title, and much else.

For several years the book remained a title without content: occasional drafts came and went but what I've written took a decade of thinking, more than 11,000 blog posts, and vast numbers of discussions to bring to life over the relatively short period in which it was eventually written.

Who else to thank then? Two colleagues stand out. The first is John Christensen, the director of the Tax Justice Network. We have been on an amazing journey together over the last twelve or so years. And then there is Colin Hines who is the convener of the Green New Deal Group, without whom many of the ideas I have promoted on the broader economic agenda would not have been cajoled into life. Both have been true friends during my campaigning career who have enriched my life far beyond the matters referred to in this book.

Academic colleagues Ronen Palan, Prem Sikka, Anastasia Nesvetailova and Sol Picciotto (professors all) demanded I improve my thinking over the years and each challenged me to go further than I had ever considered I might. I am grateful. As with all others mentioned in this introduction, none have any responsibility for the ideas and errors in this book, which, for better or worse, are all mine.

Howard Reed has been a friend and inspiration on many an occasion: it would be great to do more together. The members of the Green New Deal Group are all also due thanks: they know who they are, with Andrew Simms and Ann Pettifor standing out for special mention.

Some persistent commentators on the Tax Research UK blog, and most especially Ivan Horrocks and Andrew Dickie, encouraged me in my moderating of thousands of comments when that has, on occasion, been a thankless task. I am grateful for their moments of enlightenment.

My friends in Jersey may be surprised that I offer a note of thanks to the politicians of that island who started teaching me about obstinacy in the face of the inevitable from 2005 onwards. I'm not sure they will appreciate my thanks. Nor will the many internet trolls who have over the years taught me about the reality of politics in the social media era, even if they never once offered a single useful contribution to the debate.

I owe an enormous debt to those who have funded my work. The trustees of the Joseph Rowntree Charitable Trust showed confidence in me for five years, as did Stephen Pittam and Nick Perks, successive secretaries to that trust. That we shared our Quaker beliefs may have helped. Chapter 6 reflects that fact, unashamedly.

The TUC, PCS and Unite all offered support, work and friendship when needed. I am proud to be a chartered accountant and a trade unionist.

Many NGOs also chipped in on the way: occasionally with work, often with support. Christian Aid, Oxfam and Action Aid jump out from the crowd.

My colleagues at the Fair Tax Mark have put up with my variable input whilst the book has been in progress. My special thanks go to Meesha Nehru.

I suspect my agent, Carrie Karnia, and editor at Transworld, Doug Young, shared the doubts of many that this book would ever materialize. But they stuck with it, and the rush with which it has come into being. I look forward to repeating the process with the next idea.

No one deserves more thanks than my wife, Jacqueline, and my sons, James and Thomas. Jacqueline suffered considerable ill health during the gestation period for this book: that it was written as her recovery has progressed is the clearest indication of the way she has been integral to my work.

James and Thomas motivate me. Every morning I wake up thinking that if I have one thing to do it is to make the world a better place for them, their friends and all of their generation. Ultimately they will have to judge whether anything I have said or done has helped achieve that goal. Whatever their eventual view might be this book is for them, with my thanks for becoming the friends to me that both now are, from a father who can never really complain about how much time they spend on their computers because I have always been there just a bit longer.

Richard Murphy
Downham Market
September 2015

1
Tax and society

It has been said that the only two things in life that are inevitable are death and taxes. I hate to disappoint from the outset, but this is, very obviously, not true.

Death has indeed been inevitable from the moment that life was first known on earth. Life has, apparently, existed for about 3.5 billion years.[1] However, since as far as we know taxation is a relatively recent human invention, for approximately 3,493,000,000 years death might have been inevitable but taxation was not, because humans have been around for at most 7 million years.[2]

However, even that is too generous, because written records have existed for a mere 4,500 years and it is only from those records that we know about tax. Thus taxation may have existed for a lot less time than humans have been around. After all, there's a fair chance that tax was not the first idea we humans hit upon. So Benjamin Franklin's famous comment about tax is incorrect: for most of human existence taxation has not been inevitable. In truth most things that are said about taxation are just wrong. This will be a recurring theme of this book.

It is, however, worth noting that we do have written records from about 2500 BC and that some of the earliest, from Mesopotamia, record that tax was a part of life back then, just as it is now.[3] From this it would seem that, while taxes may not be inevitable, they have been a fixture on the agenda of humankind ever since we tried to live in any form of complex society. If that's what Benjamin Franklin meant then we can let him off with his error for the remaining 3,499,995,500 years of living history.

The history of taxation is, in fact, important. If we are to understand what we want from taxation now – and that will be another recurring theme of this book – then we have to be sure that we're not just reinventing that history and what it has to tell us. That's why I am concentrating on this issue in this first chapter.

Most histories of tax start in the modern era, but it was actually the Babylonians who are the first known to be in on the act despite having some problems to overcome in achieving their aims. In particular they had the slight difficulty that there was no money available to settle tax debt. The relationship between money and tax is of enormous significance, as Chapter 3 will explain, but back then paying tax involved payment in kind. That could be in goods. So, payment in sheep and cows was possible. But so too was payment with your own labour; that was the first form of income tax. It is also apparent that other levies such as tariffs on imports and exports existed, paid with a part of the cargo, whilst in 1900 BC there is a record of a person being imprisoned for smuggling. Tax evasion has evidently been on the scene for a very long time.

Babylon might be the first place that we know had taxes, but the idea definitely spread. The Bible, and most especially the Old Testament, provides some very clear references to taxation, even if it does not always mention the word as such.[4] It talks of personal levies (or a poll tax)[5] and taxes on land.[6] It also suggests that they were to be paid in grain,[7] or in provisions.[8] And there was, of course, the whole process of tithing, which looks remarkably like an income tax.[9]

In other cases the whole issue of proportionality and the ability to pay is considered. So, for example, in 2 Kings[10] it is said that tax was only to be taken from 'the men of substance', while elsewhere in the same book[11] it is said that Jehoiakim 'exacted the silver and gold from the people of the land, from each proportionately', though frustratingly we are not told what, precisely, that might mean. Read together, however, the suggestion that capacity to pay and progressive taxation might have been on the tax agenda thousands of years ago is intriguing.

The Romans had many bases for charging taxes. The first preferred taxes were land-based, but these were abolished in Rome itself in 167 BC because the proceeds of expansion of the empire rendered them unnecessary.[12] This was not true elsewhere, especially later in the life of the empire, by which times fortunes had changed considerably.[13] Poll taxes based on land ownership remained popular with Roman administrators throughout the provinces. There were also customs duties and tolls, and special taxes on trading slaves. Extraordinarily, inheritance taxes at the rate of 5 per cent were charged at one time on those who did not leave property to their families.

In the later history of the Roman Empire sales taxes were more common and so too was resistance. It is thought that the revolt of Boudicca may have been related to tax demands,[14] and it is widely suggested that the refusal of Rome's wealthy elites to pay the tax that they owed helped bring the empire to an end.

The tale of the disliked tax collector appears to have its origins in the Roman Empire. The tax collectors in the provinces, much referred to in the New Testament (maybe as a result of one, St Matthew, becoming a disciple of Jesus), were widely despised. Jesus also made comment on tax itself, including the obligation to pay it,[15] as did St Paul.[16]

The essential point to be made from this very brief tour through history before the Dark Ages is that so many features of modern tax debate resonate in what was happening then. There were discussions on the ethics of tax, whilst attempts to find different tax bases were obviously commonplace: land, income, wealth, sales, imports and exports, and simply being alive and having been counted (poll taxes) were all tried out at various times. There were also more methods of settlement than today, where payment in kind is rarely an option. And, lest we think they are modern inventions, there were also allowances, exemptions for special economic circumstances, and wealthy people who got out of or simply refused to pay the taxes they owed.

In the background to all this there is also a theme of resentment. The resentment of having to pay tax to an authority imposed upon them that led to the rebellion of the Iceni tribe in Britain was no doubt little different to that of the first-century Jews as reported in the New Testament. Innovation in ways of collecting tax resulting in conflict and dispute appears to be a part of the history of the period. Through it all, though, there is a recurring theme, which is that governments (or, at least, the autocratic and often foreign rulers who represented government in this era) needed cash to fund their military and territorial ambitions, and tax was a way of getting it.

It is a theme that survived the Dark Ages. William I of England may have wanted an inventory of the wealth of the land he'd conquered in 1066, but there is no doubt that the resulting Domesday Book was not just a record of curiosity; it was also a basis for tax assessment of the people now subject to his rule. Issues relating to taxation, and its imposition, have constantly been a significant factor in the history of many countries, of which England is simply an example.

There is good reason for this. The ability to tax is an exercise in economic power over others. This fact is inescapable. At the heart of much, if not most, conflict over the last thousand years has been dispute over who should have that power over which other people. It is a primal dispute that is still at the core of politics today. All that has changed over time is, it could be argued, who has been disputing this issue, over what territory, with which intended outcome.

For example, the major constitutional disputes in the UK's history have always revolved around this issue. Within 34 years of William I conquering England his son, Henry I, had to sign a Charter of Liberties[17] to win acceptance for his reign. It is suggested one of the grievances that the English barons had with the Crown concerned taxation, although the charter itself simply pledged to uphold the rule of law.

Henry did not keep his word to the barons, but he had set a precedent that, in a sense, began a change in the direction of travel with regard to tax. His father William the Conqueror was a straightforward, old-fashioned autocratic ruler, invading a territory and imposing his right to tax by might. Henry, his son, had to grant favours, even if he had little intention of honouring them, to achieve the same objective. The dark ages of taxation could almost be said to have died just after the conquest of England.

If there was still doubt about that new process of taxation by (albeit somewhat limited) consent then Magna Carta made it clear that the era of tax by royal decree was definitely meant to have come to an end. The demand for reform that gave rise to Magna Carta was, at least in part, tax driven. Taxes had been heavy as a result of the wars of both Kings Richard and John, from which the barons had gained little. Their willingness to continue paying taxes for wars from which they did not gain was limited. Their threat of rebellion brought the era of tax without representation to an official end.

Signed in 1215, the Magna Carta contained two significant clauses relating to tax. Clause 12 required that the king accept the 'common counsel of our kingdom' when levying and assessing an aid or a scutage, which would now be called a tax.[18] Clause 14 tried to specify what that process of common counsel meant and required that the archbishops, bishops, abbots, earls and greater barons should be consulted on any tax matter.[19] It is curious that the clause 13 that divided these two said:

> *And the city of London is to have all its ancient*
> *liberties and free customs, both on land and*
> *water.*

It is extraordinary that even in the thirteenth century the City had to have its rights stated plumb in the middle of a consideration on how tax might be lawfully imposed. Some may say little has changed since then.

With or without the City, it is fair to say that clauses 12 and 14 of the Magna Carta were, firstly, a revolution in the legal basis for the right to tax and, secondly, were probably much more ignored than they were ever complied with. Nevertheless the precedent that they set was what mattered. There was in these clauses a specific constraint on the right of the king – the executive government of the day – to tax without consultation with representatives of the country at large. Those representatives may not have been very representative, but the change was definite. The right to tax without representation had been eroded for the first time. In many ways the history of the following 800 years in the UK is just a footnote to the principle established in Magna Carta: the whole argument on constitutional reform since 1215 might be said to be about who was to be represented in discussion on the right to tax, in what area, and when.

What is clear is that there was a feeling that Magna Carta gave too few the right to be heard. De Montfort's parliament of 1265 extended the right of representation on some issues – but not it appears on tax – to some who were not peers. Another precedent had been set, but it took until 1362 for a statute to be passed that required the consent of the people of the realm before the king could tax their lands and goods.[20]

Taxation and representation had become inextricably linked in England but that did not, of course, satisfy everyone. England might have had a parliament but it represented the interests of a tiny minority in society, being made up of peers, senior clergy, and commoners who were mainly knights and members of the landed class. This did not go unnoticed by those left out of the equation. Wat Tyler's Peasants' Revolt of 1381 was triggered by the attempts made by a royal official, John Bampton, to collect unpaid poll taxes in the town of Brentwood in Essex. The rebellion may not have lasted long, and 1,500 of those who were involved were executed for expressing their opinion on tax in such fashion, but it clearly demonstrated that tax was an emotive topic, and that the grant of representation to some gave rise to similar expectation amongst others. The genie was out of the bottle.

It was a subject that was, eventually, to come to a head in the reign of King Charles I of England, Scotland and Ireland. There is little doubt that Charles was not a very wise man. He inflamed passion on many issues and as a result did his very best not to consult the English parliament. Having fallen into dispute with Parliament, and having then dissolved it three times between 1625 and 1629, he resolved to rule without it, whatever the statute of 1362 had to say regarding his obligation to consult Parliament on matters relating to taxation.

And tax was at the heart of the differences of opinion. Parliament did not trust a monarch married to a Catholic. They reflected this mistrust in a refusal to grant Charles the right to collect tonnage and poundage (two forms of customs duty) for more than a year at a time. Tax was thus being used as a weapon in a power conflict. A parliament seeking one form of society sought to deny revenue to a king who they thought wanted another type of society altogether. The idea was emerging that tax might influence and reflect the society a country both was and wanted to be.

Charles would have none of this. In his opinion it was his opinion that mattered; that was his God-given right. His problem was, however, that there was by the seventeenth century no obvious divine right to raise tax without parliamentary approval. Despite this he ruled for eleven years without a parliament. During that period he could, legally, resort only to his customary rights and prerogatives to raise tax. So he did, for example, force those earning more than £40 a year to be knighted and to pay for the privilege. But, most of all, he relied on 'ship money', a privilege tax supposedly to pay for the navy but which Charles used to supplement the tonnage and poundage that he was collecting illegally. Land taxes – enforced by extension of the royal forests in England and by revocation of gifts of land in Scotland and replacing them with rents – were further attempts to raise revenue without parliamentary consent.

It cannot be said the outcome of all this was inevitable. There had never before been a revolution of the type that England had undergone by 1649. What can be said with certainty is that tax was a central, if not the sole, cause of this enormous constitutional upset in English history. What is also clear is that the aftermath of Charles's death and the creation of a Commonwealth under Cromwell did not solve all the problems. Indeed, Cromwell's relationship with Parliament was on occasion little better than Charles's had been, and by 1660 the monarchy had been re-established.

Things were not, however, ever the same again. The relationship of trust between King and Parliament had been fatally undermined. In the Glorious Revolution of 1688–9, when Charles's son, James II, was effectively overthrown to be replaced by William and Mary, who accepted the throne at the invitation of Parliament, the balance of power irrevocably shifted. William and Mary had to consent to a Declaration of Rights before accepting the throne. Among other things this prohibited taxation without parliamentary consent. By 1694 a demand for regular parliaments was backed up by the Triennial Act.

* * *

The road from Babylon to London in 1694 is a long one: maybe 4,000 years of taxation history leading to this fundamental shift in the balance of power, in England at least. No longer could the English monarch tax at will; an effective limit on taxation by prerogative had been created by a parliament that, albeit very incompletely, represented the people of the country. Magna Carta established a precedent that the Charter of Liberties had failed to achieve; now the Glorious Revolution established another ground rule that the more violent revolution of the Civil Wars had failed to deliver. Never again, in England, would there be taxation without some form of representation. The gauntlet had in effect been thrown down by England's Parliament and an example had been created for all societies. A threat had been established for all monarchs. Since 1689 tax has been at the core of social revolution.

Thus it was that in Britain's American colonies the cry went up of 'no taxation without representation' at the time of the Boston Tea Party in 1773. This was a straightforward rejection of the Tea Act passed by what was, by then, the British Parliament, which was meant to enforce the obligation on Americans to buy tea on which duty had been paid. The attempt to impose a tax from afar on tea was a trigger point. The developing American colonies were no longer willing to accept taxation imposed without their consent. The Declaration of

Independence followed in 1776. In the list of complaints that, in the eyes of those signing the Declaration, justified their actions, was one statement of grievance about the King which was as short as it was unambiguous: they said that he had consented to 'Acts of pretended Legislation . . . For imposing Taxes on us without our Consent'.[21]

It is possible that no one grievance has been more important in the demands that people have made when seeking their independence. Roll forward 240 years and the Scots' bid in 2014 to seek independence from the rest of the United Kingdom. On page 2 of the Scottish government's case for independence it argued that 'we have generated more tax receipts per person than the UK for every one of the last 30 years. We are in a fiscally stronger position than the rest of the UK.'[22] The point being made was clear: the Scots had raised more money themselves than the rest of the UK, and they wanted control of it. National pride, long-term differences of view that have meant Scotland and England have never truly integrated, and different cultures might all have impacted on Scotland's claim to become the newest country in the world, but when it came down to it debate was really about one thing, and that was, to use the phrase coined by James Carville, Bill Clinton's election adviser in 1992, 'the economy, stupid'. What is more, 'the economy, stupid' very clearly meant control of tax and spending.

The Bostonians of 1773 and the Scottish government of 2014 were not alone in realizing this. The Americans were just ahead of the French in understanding that to wrest control of taxation and spending from an authority out of sympathy with the will of a nation was the pre-requisite of change, and, in the case of France, the precursor of revolution. At the core of the French uprising in 1789 was a demand for the overthrow of feudalism and the privileges and taxes that maintained it. Even if 'Liberté, Égalité, Fraternité' was not, in fact, the cry of that revolution, in the Age of Enlightenment it was held self-evident that taxation not only had to reflect society, but had the capacity to change society. It may not have been coincidence that Adam Smith published his theory of taxation in his book *The Wealth of Nations* in 1776, the year the United States of America declared independence from Britain.

Another paradigm in taxation had shifted. It was becoming clear that nation states were defined by their ability to tax and that the credibility of those states was, albeit rather hesitantly at first, being determined by their willingness to tax in accordance with the views of those who were governed. As the Scots proved in 2014, arguments about the limits of the state, and its right to tax, still go on today. But what may not have been antici-pated in the USA in 1776 or in France in 1789 is just what representation might come to mean.

Some contemporaries of the French revolution, like

Thomas Paine, were arguing for universal male suffrage, but they were way ahead of their time, and those who argued for women's suffrage were even more so. The Enlightenment was not that enlightened as yet, but matters were to change. Although the linkage between tax and the creation of universal suffrage is too complex to explore in detail, it is clear that the relationship exists. It comes down, quite simply, to the old adage of 'no taxation without representation', and as the demands on modern states grew so too did suffrage, including, over time, that for women. Despite that it is curious, and embarrassing to note, that in the UK it was only in 1988 that the income of married women ceased to be declared on their husband's tax returns as if it were his property.[23] Taxation has sometimes changed to influence social mores. At other times it has been dragged into reflecting them.

This brief review of the history of taxation shows, I suggest, a number of things.

The first is that like it or not tax is a part of any society. Let's not fight it then; let's embrace it instead.

Secondly, many of the questions relating to tax that we struggle with now have been around ever since tax was first charged in ancient times. Questions such as who to charge it on, based on what economic activity, at what rate and whether that rate might vary depending on the circumstances of the taxpayer have existed for as long as people have recorded their history. So too have issues relating to allowances and reliefs; while tax evasion has been around from the start as if (as seems likely) it is inseparable from tax itself.

Thirdly, tax may be accepted (which clearly it usually was; after all, the states and empires that imposed it did seem to enjoy remarkable durability), but can also give rise to substantial tensions, and on occasion to outright revolt. There is, however, what appears to be a common theme to these ancient revolts that seems to have extended right through to the modern era, and even the present day. Tax is accepted if the authority imposing it appears to reflect the society that is paying it. Of course that process of reflection has changed over time, as has the number of people brought within the scope of the tax net, but this issue has been constant. Tax and society appear to be inextricably linked.

As a consequence tax has been integral to the process of the development of the modern state, which is in very many respects defined by its ability to tax in a way acceptable to those living within its domain – failing which it is forcibly broken up, as the American colonies once proved to Britain and as the Scots tried, only slightly less convincingly, to do recently.

Tax has also been integral to the development of the process of democracy. Without the demand for representation on the issue of taxation it is very unlikely that the currently preferred method of government in a great many states in the world would exist.

The result is broader than the history implies, though. The implication of these conclusions is that the history of tax is little less than the history of the state itself.[24] After all, it is taxes that define in no small part what a state thinks it can do. And it is the consent of the people to that process of taxation that does in turn limit or empower the capacity of a state to act. Without that consent a state is restricted in how it can protect and provide for those within its borders. The fortunes of a people are, therefore, intimately linked to this process of consensual taxation.

It is only one step on from that realization to appreciate that tax both provides the basis for the power of a state and at the same time binds the people and the state in which they live together. That, though, can only happen with representation. And because representation appears to be related to the demand to pay, tax is in fact central to the creation of good government. We cannot, quite literally, do without it if we are to prosper, as the fate of so many states that can rely on oil revenues alone, without demands for other taxes being necessary, appears to prove.

This idea does, of course, build on Rousseau's idea of the social contract. I think there is such a contract between the people of a nation and their government. And the consideration in that contract is the tax that is paid. That tax must reflect the values and priorities of those people. If it does people will willingly pay it and return the government that charges it to power. If it does not reflect those values they can, in a democracy, change that government, and will. This process of choice is then enabled by tax and democracy working hand in hand. We can get good government and we can make that government reflect our will and needs precisely because they want the tax that we pay, whether or not they could raise funds by other means (which is an issue to which I will return later). It is this vibrant and symbiotic relationship, developed over a long time and reflecting the struggle of many people to deliver it, that is, in my opinion, the first Joy of Tax.

2

What is tax?

For most people tax means income tax. If you were to listen solely to the media and politicians when they talk about tax that is what they are really referring to. So, for example, there was a headline in the UK's *Daily Telegraph* in February 2013 that said 'Top 14 per cent of taxpayers pay 60 per cent of all tax'.[1] Except they don't, of course. The tax referred to was income tax, and that's a long way from being all the tax paid in this country, or any other country come to that.

For the record, in the 2013/14 tax year it is thought that the total tax take in the UK was as shown in Figure 1.

I hope that this straight away shatters the myth that there is only one sort of tax. That is very obviously untrue.

I also hope it shatters the myth that the only tax that really matters is income tax. It isn't. Income tax represents only just over a quarter of all taxes paid in the UK. That's a lot, but it's not all taxes.

Figure 1: UK taxes in the 2013–14 tax year

HM Revenue & Customs	£'billion	% of total tax
Income tax (gross of tax credits)	155.0	27.3%
Tax credits (negative tax)	−2.7	−0.5%
National insurance contributions	106.9	18.8%
Value added tax	105.1	18.5%
Corporation tax	40.1	7.1%
Corporation tax credits	−1.0	−0.2%
Petroleum revenue tax	1.1	0.2%
Fuel duties	26.8	4.7%
Capital gains tax	3.9	0.7%
Inheritance tax	3.5	0.6%
Stamp duty land tax	9.5	1.7%
Stamp taxes on shares	3.1	0.5%
Tobacco duties	9.6	1.7%
Spirits duties	3.0	0.5%
Wine duties	3.7	0.7%
Beer and cider duties	3.6	0.6%
Air passenger duty	3.0	0.5%
Insurance premium tax	3.1	0.5%
Climate change levy	1.0	0.2%
Landfill tax	1.2	0.2%
Aggregates levy	0.3	0.1%
Betting and gaming duties	2.1	0.4%
Customs duties	2.9	0.5%
Bank levy	2.2	0.4%
Swiss capital tax	0.6	0.1%
Total HMRC	487.7	85.8%
Vehicle excise duties	6.1	1.1%
Business rates	26.8	4.7%
Council tax	26.8	4.7%
VAT refunds	13.9	2.4%
EU ETS Auction Receipts	0.3	0.1%
Other taxes and royalties	6.9	1.2%
Total net taxes and NICs	568.6	100.0%

Source: Office for Budget Responsibility, Budget reports March 2014[2]

Lastly I hope it shatters the myth that the most affluent pay most of the tax raised in the UK. Of course they pay a lot of tax. That is because they have a much higher income and/or much greater accumulated wealth than most people, which inevitably means they pay more than most people do in, for instance, income tax; but it is not the case, as the *Daily Telegraph* claimed, that they pay 60 per cent of all taxes. For example, they probably pay little more in fuel duty than most other people with a car do. And in proportion to their income they pay less council tax than most in the UK because the maximum that anyone can pay is capped for the purposes of that tax.

This is a theme I will return to, but there are two important points to make here.

The first is that we have lots of taxes.

The second is that people don't always tell the truth about tax.

Part of my aim in writing this book is to cut away some of that untruth. And I will also try to make clear when what I am offering is opinion, based on my interpretation of facts, which is more than the *Daily Telegraph*'s headline did.

So, what then is tax, which is the question I am meant to be addressing. According to the online Oxford dictionary it is:

> *A compulsory contribution to state revenue,*
> *levied by the government on workers' income*

and business profits, or added to the cost of some goods, services, and transactions.[3]

This is, I am afraid to say, despite the authority of the source, about as misleading as the *Daily Telegraph*'s headline quoted above. For a start we do not now only charge tax on 'workers'' incomes (a phrase itself suggestive of a deeply class-based system) and profits; we also charge tax on income from invested savings, pensions and rents. We can and do also charge tax on wealth, as we do in the case of inheritance tax, or on gains, as is the case with capital gains tax, or on occupation of property, as council taxes do, and in exchange for services, as landfill tax does. The collective term for all this is 'the tax base'. The tax base is made up of the things on which we want to charge tax. Any definition of tax can, and should, make reference to the tax base, but that still does not define what tax is because the tax base can exist without being taxed (as a lot of land does in the UK right now). So they're not the same.

Next, the Oxford Dictionary definition states baldly that tax is 'a compulsory contribution to state revenue'. There are, however, major problems with this view. As I have sought to show in Chapter 1, the whole history of tax, government and democracy is entangled precisely because those who have been taxed have demanded that their consent to taxation be sought before any such charge was imposed. In that case is it true to say that there is 'compulsion'? Even if it is undoubtedly true that a great many people in modern democracies are disenchanted with modern politics they do have the right to vote in elections that result in the formation of the governments that set the taxes in the countries in which they reside. Compulsion is hard to suggest in that case.

What is more, those same people also have a right to try to influence the democratic process. They can either do that directly by actually standing for election or by supporting those who do, or they can do it indirectly, by seeking to influence ideas, as I am in writing this book. So, the suggestion conveyed by 'compulsory contribution', that people are excluded from the tax-making process which is then imposed upon them, has to be challenged.

Finally, and for the sake of the record, many people in the UK and many other countries do have a right to leave the country if they really do feel they are being compelled to do something they do not want. That's not true of everyone, but the evidence that people actually move for tax reasons is very limited indeed.[4] Again, the idea of compulsion is hard to sustain.

Instead, and implicit in this notion of compulsion, what the Oxford definition actually embraces is the idea that government is itself imposed upon us and if only we could we would opt out of it. I do not accept that view. There are remarkably few examples of states without governments. It is true that Belgium survived without a government for nineteen months in 2010–11,[5] but the machinery of state continued despite that because it was always assumed a government would return. There are also places that do not have effective government. However, few would choose to live in parts of Somalia, Iraq, Syria, and the like. In fact, the absence of government is usually the precursor to or consequence of profoundly unattractive situations deeply prejudicial to human well-being. Government is therefore, I suggest, not imposed but willingly accepted by the vast majority as a matter of choice. That is because most of us instinctively think it a 'good thing'. The idea that government is 'imposed' on us is simply not true in a functioning democracy. We actively consent to its operation and if we do not get the government we want then it is, at least potentially, our fault for not doing something about it.[6]

What of tax then? Is tax accepted as a matter of choice by those making payment of it? There is evidence to suggest that it is.

First of all, when taxes are considered deeply unacceptable then this sentiment is very loudly and clearly conveyed. One of the best examples in recent history occurred in the UK. In 1989 the Conservative government of Margaret Thatcher introduced what it described as a Community Charge but which was almost universally described by everyone else as a poll tax. This poll tax was designed to replace the local taxation system that had been linked to capacity to pay inasmuch as it was based on the value of a property a person owned, and thus a form of wealth tax. The Community Charge instead required payment of a single flat-rate per-capita tax by every adult living in a local authority area, with only limited credit for those with very low incomes. So strong was opposition to this poll tax that rioting actually preceded its introduction in England and Wales (it had first been introduced into Scotland) including a major outbreak in London in March 1990.[7] So clear was feeling on this issue, and so damaged was the government by it, that by November 1990 Margaret Thatcher had been ousted from office by her own political party.

The message of this incident is very plain: however much we may grumble, the reality is that tax is actually imposed by consent, and is also paid by consent. Indeed, one reason why the poll tax headed for extinction so quickly was that in some areas there was simply insufficient court capacity to enforce recovery of the tax or to penalize those refusing to comply with demands for payment. That was unprecedented. If it occurred on a regular basis with other taxes the UK's system of justice would collapse remarkably quickly.

According to HM Revenue & Customs 90 per cent of all tax is paid without 'HMRC doing anything'.[8] Whilst I do not entirely agree (since they do have to send out reminders to pay in the first instance and administer the system), I think there is a strong element of truth to that suggestion if they mean that most tax is paid with little or no further intervention on their part. It follows that, in contrast with the reaction to the poll tax, the vast majority of tax is paid by consent in this country, and I suspect that is also true around much of the world.

There may be good reason for that consent. The graph in Figure 2 shows the relationship between nominal GDP (gross domestic product) per head of population in

Figure 2: Aggregate tax rate compared with nominal GDP per capita in 175 countries in 2013

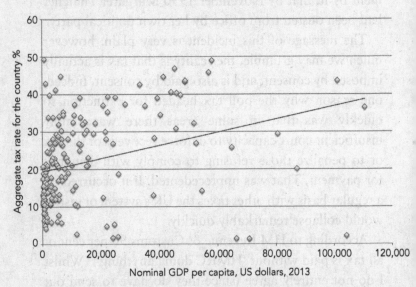

Source: author's calculations based on data from the CIA Factbook and the Heritage Foundation (see notes 9 and 10)

175 countries according to the CIA Factbook (a reliable source)[9] and aggregate taxation as a proportion of that GDP (source: the Heritage Foundation, which seems reliable on this occasion).[10] I added the linear trend line.

The graph shows that as GDP per capita rises so does the aggregate tax rate. Or vice versa, of course. The relationship holds if countries with a per capita GDP below $5,000 a year, $10,000 and $20,000 a year are excluded, although the trend line begins to flatten a little as the rate of exclusion increases, perhaps unsurprisingly.

I also tested the relationship by excluding states with very low tax rates (often tax havens or places heavily dependent upon oil revenues) from the sample. If countries with aggregate tax rates of less than 10 per cent are excluded, the relationship is very strong: as tax rates rise so does GDP per capita markedly increase on average. Even when considering countries with aggregate tax rates of over 39 per cent (the UK's rate) (but with Zimbabwe excluded as an aberration in the data) the relationship is positive, i.e. income still rises with the aggregate tax rate.

Now that does not of itself prove anything – correlation is not proof of causation – but it does seem to suggest that higher-taxed states are better off, and it's my suspicion that most people know this. They realize that there is in fact a relationship between tax and well-being and that it is strongly positive for a country and so, in turn, for them. And that is why, as HM Revenue & Customs have put it, the vast majority of tax is paid without them having to do (almost) anything.

If that is true, and if it is also true that tax charges are created by consent in a modern democracy with a universal franchise, then the view of tax that the Oxford Dictionary presents, and which would be widely recognized by a great many people, is not just wrong, it is actually a complete misrepresentation of the truth in the situation described. In fact, the Oxford Dictionary is in pretty much the same place as the *Daily Telegraph* was when talking about the proportion of tax paid by the rich: spinning a line that is deeply misleading.

That is not to say there is no element of compulsion to tax. It would be impossible to deny that there is, but when saying that we have a duty to ask why that compulsion exists and not just treat it as if it is an essential feature of the system, when it isn't. In truth, the compulsion is there because compulsion is a usual sanction that society imposes on behaviour that society thinks aberrant. In other words, society actually treats compliance (voluntary payment of tax) as normal and only requires compulsion to deal with those who break that convention. Let's think about other areas where sanctions for aberrant behaviour exist. We do, for example, have laws to penalize burglary but not because most of us want to steal. That, I am pretty sure, is just not the case.

The law sanctioning theft as unacceptable behaviour is there because a few people within society do commit burglary despite the very obvious fact that the vast majority of us think that it is wrong to steal from someone else.

The same logic should be applied to the sanctions the law imposes with regard to tax. Just as most of us voluntarily refrain from burglary without the requirement of any law to tell us not to do so, so do most of us in a modern democracy voluntarily pay our tax. It is for those who break the norm of society, by refusing to comply with what most of us think is the right thing to do, that we have law that penalizes anyone who persists in doing the wrong thing. The fact that we have these laws and use them relatively rarely (as the poll tax experience proves) is not evidence of compulsion but the exact opposite, which is that compliance is the norm that needs to be enforced only exceptionally.

If that is true, then to put compulsion at the start of the definition of tax – as the Oxford Dictionary has, and as many people do – is absurd in the *current* political context. I stress 'current' for good reason, since of course this has not always been true. It made sense in the four-teenth century for the peasants to revolt: they did not set the taxes that it was demanded they pay. Indeed, the same grievance had earlier motivated the barons to demand Magna Carta. And it may equally have made sense for people to object to the Community Charge, a tax imposed by a government clearly out of touch with the sentiment of the people it was governing and which acted contrary to the principles of economic fairness many think inherent in democracy, which is a logic that flows from its deep associations with taxation and the sense that a tax is only fair if it reflects the capacity of a person to pay it. By that reasoning, the poll tax protests were against something seen as anti-democratic, and not the tax as such. This same logic also, no doubt, explains the Scottish nationalists' demand for the Scottish parliament to have the right to determine taxes and spending, to reflect their society which appears to them to be clearly different from that of the UK as a whole.

All that being noted, however, in most times and in most cases it has to be said that this need to resort to violent protest about tax is unnecessary. We have the mechanisms to put forward our views and to change and reform taxation to suit the society we want and respect: that is the democratic process at work. And, as I have argued in Chapter 1, that democratic process owes its existence to tax. The notion that tax is compulsorily imposed is anachronistic and should be a remnant of another age, when one class imposed their will on others who were not represented in the decision-making process. Now that we are, or at least can be (although some shamefully absent themselves from it), a part of that decision-making process, tax is not imposed but is consensual.

What follows on quite logically from that realization is the understanding that tax paid does not become the property of some alien body. It is the property of a government in which we have a stake, and in which we participate.

The consequences of this understanding are radical. Government is not now some 'other being' over which we have no control. It is something that we want to exist and in whose operation we consent. That's not to say that at the same time we do not also understand that government is different from us: the democratic process clearly creates the possibility that there will be governments and taxes that we personally would never have supported with our vote. We do, however, consent none the less to comply with them because within the democratic process we accept the consequence of a will greater than our own. We are in one sense a part of government because we vote for it and so hope to have influence and even some control over its actions. And yet at the same time we also consent when it does not do what we want. And when that happens we realize that government has an existence apart from us and that we also consent to this. These two positions are, of course, in ever-present tension with each other, but that is the basis of the political process in a democracy. Both opinions most definitely exist, and simultaneously.

This realization has enormous significance for the debate on what tax is. If we consent to the existence of government and willingly consent to its right to tax, then another phrase in popular use is also profoundly incorrect: every time a politician says they are spending taxpayers' money (and they do, often, even dedicating whole speeches to it[11]) they are making another statement that is simply untrue. Tax is not taxpayers' money. It is the government's money and it is the government's rightful property. It is absurd to claim otherwise.

First of all this is because if tax really were taxpayers' money then the government would have no right to spend it; yet it very obviously has that right, not least because we gave it that right. And then there is the fact that tax is, of course, legally defined as the property of government, which is why when consent fails it can enforce its claim to ownership of it. What is more, this property right of the government, which results in its claim that it owns tax, has been created in exactly the same way as all other property in a modern democracy, which is by statute law. It is also enforced in the same way, through the courts. In that case for politicians to then pretend that this property right of the government to own funds paid in tax does not exist because the cash involved is still in some way 'taxpayers' money' is not just wrong, it is profoundly misleading. It is also, and at least as importantly, a denial of their responsibility for that money. That's not encouraging.

Second, if the funds really were the property of taxpayers, as this statement suggests, then the government would merely act as agent for the people of a jurisdiction and not have an existence in its own right. There is a libertarian view that holds this to be true, just as that view also claims (when it is convenient to those making the argument) that companies registered by law are nothing more than a bundle of contracts and that they have no real existence. Both arguments, however, stretch credibility beyond any reasonable limit.

That's partly because governments and companies can and do own property, and can and do decide how and where resources will be used, and in ways that cannot be attributable to the acts of any one individual. That is a sure sign of decidedly separate existence from any one person, let alone any one taxpayer. This point then suggests the second reason why the argument that government is just an agent for taxpayers is wrong: it is a matter of fact that any government (or company, come to that) is more than the sum of its parts and to suggest they are mere contractual arrangements or agents for the people they supposedly represent is, therefore, wrong. They have existence over, above and beyond that. It takes an extraordinary leap of imagination to think otherwise; the same sort of leap that permits a person to believe in the tooth fairy when an adult.

At which point, and having made all these observations as to what is wrong with current perceptions of tax, the time has come to put something in their place. Based on these observations that government exists with our consent, and because it is clear that it has a legal right to the ownership of property to which we have also consented, and because we might sometimes have possession of part of that property which rightfully belongs to the government (which as a matter of fact many of us do because we receive some or all of our income without tax being deducted), then the action that we call paying tax is actually the process by which we transfer to the government that part of the funds that we hold which rightfully are not ours but are in fact the property of the state.

Or, to put it another way, the idea that tax is our money that the government holds on our behalf is completely wrong. Tax is actually the government's money that we sometimes hold on its behalf. That's the exact opposite of what most politicians currently claim but in a modern democracy it is hard to see how any other conclusion is possible. To put it more formally:

> *In a democracy with a universal franchise that provides every adult with a right to seek election, tax is that property held in trust by an individual or company that is due to the state whose rightful and legal property it is.*

I stress that this is not in any way a definition that challenges the right to own private property. In fact the exact opposite is the case. Because the government's right to claim the tax that it owns is a property right, just like any other, defining tax in this way reinforces the property right of everyone in a society and says everyone has the right to own what is really theirs. What is more, given that a democracy can only exist when property rights are upheld (because anarchy breaks out pretty quickly if they aren't), recognition of the government's property right is absolutely fundamental to the maintenance of a democracy and the contention, made by all too many politicians in recent years, that tax is not really a government's property to spend as it sees fit is, I suggest, language designed by those who do not respect either government or democracy and who want to undermine the role of both, in order to reduce the confidence we have in the state in which we live.

It's a sad fact that this rhetoric undermining the state seems to have worked. Confidence in democracy has fallen as the use of language like this has grown in recent years. The alienation it has created between us and the state of which we are a part has increased over recent decades as indicated by declining voting rates and disenchantment with the political process.

This just leaves some final comments to be made before we move on to look at more particular aspects of tax. The first is a really important and obvious conclusion to draw from the discussion I have just offered. This is that whilst we have an absolute right to own private property, that is only true if we have settled the tax that we might owe as a result of acquiring, using, selling, gifting or otherwise disposing of that property. So we do not own our gross income if the government says that tax is due as a result of acquiring it. We only own our net income. This obvious conclusion follows from the definition of tax that I have offered, but it's important to make it clear for two reasons.

The first is that this rule applies to anyone who can acquire, own, use or dispose of property. So the often suggested argument of libertarians that companies do not exist, being a mere bundle of contracts, and that therefore they cannot actually pay tax (because only real, live, warm-blooded individuals can do so) is wrong. Tax is a property right and companies quite emphatically have property rights and that means that they can and do as a result have to pay tax in their own right. The same is true of trusts (which exist independently of their trustees), charities and partnerships. The idea that tax is something that is simply of concern to individuals is just wrong. It's appropriately charged on any body with the necessary property rights.

The second significant idea that this introduces is that any attempt by an individual to reduce the property right of a state to claim the tax that is rightfully its property is an action like all others that are motivated by the desire to take from somebody something that is rightfully theirs. Such acts are at best a con trick, which is how they might be described when they fall within the law but leave the other party aggrieved and full of righteous indignation, or they are outright theft. Conventionally we have called the first of these two activities tax avoidance and the second tax evasion. But either way they're an abuse of someone else's property; in this case the government's. No wonder then that they have given rise to widespread condemnation, although precisely why that has been so has very often been hard for people to explain. That difficulty is now resolved using the understanding of tax that I have offered here.

When tax is defined as something we owe by compulsion to a government that is alien to us, out of property all of which is rightfully our own, then the claim can be made that tax avoidance and tax evasion are actions to prevent our own property being taken from us by duress. This affords cover to the tax abuser and those who assist them in their activities. No wonder they are so keen on the type of definition of tax found in the Oxford Dictionary. Such a definition even lets them claim they're doing a socially just act by preventing their property being taken from them – except for just one little problem, which is that such claims have very obviously been an affront to millions and millions of people in recent years, including, apparently, those very same politicians who have told us that all they do is spend taxpayers' money.

And that affront does, in itself, very strongly suggest that what I have argued in this chapter is right. We are offended by those who claim they have a right to avoid tax. That is because most of us know that we are not alienated from government: the vast majority of us feel that to at least some degree our interests and its are closely aligned and that because of our power to participate in the democratic process, action to abuse the government is also action to abuse us. This is why we are so passionate on this issue: we think that to take what is rightfully the property of government is an act that abuses us all, which of course it is.

That's why there has been public outcry on tax, but it only makes sense if tax is defined in the way I suggest it should be here. And because the outcry indicates most people do feel a sentiment that can only be explained in this way then I suggest the majority will also share this view of tax.

That's not to say some won't disagree. But to go back to an example noted earlier: to ask burglars to both define the law of theft and at the same time to shape public opinion on the issue because they are the self-proclaimed experts on the subject would, I think, by common consent be considered unwise. We should take the same view of the supposed tax specialists whose expertise is largely based on their prowess in denying the state access to its rightful property. In a democracy a consensus should be defined by the majority. On tax we have got that wrong and have instead accepted a minority view and it is time to correct that now.

The reality is that in a democracy tax can be seen to be one of the cleverest of human inventions, and one from which we all benefit as a result of the massive contribution it makes to our well-being. No wonder I think there's a Joy to Tax.

3

Why we tax

Why does a government tax? The answer may seem
blindingly obvious: to raise money to meet its planned
expenditure. However, it's a simple fact that, completely
contrary to popular perception, no government has to
charge tax to be able to spend on what it wants to do.
Most governments usually choose to raise taxes, but other
mechanisms *are* open to them to achieve their spending
goals. These need to be understood before considering
why they use tax when there are alternatives available.

The most obvious practicable alternative to tax is for
a government to print money to pay for its expenditure.
As a matter of fact, although many like to deny it,
modern governments do often do this so that they might
meet the expectations they have raised among their
electorate as to the services they will offer in exchange
for their votes.

Many people seem to think this money-printing exercise an extraordinary idea, no doubt influenced by the fact that a lot of economists argue that money-printing should not happen because it will, in their opinion, always debase a country's currency, with inflation running out of control as a consequence. Experience has, however, shown that this need not be the case. For example in the UK, where between March 2009 and July 2012 the Bank of England bought £375 billion of UK government debt in the London financial markets[1] in an exercise technically described as quantitative easing but which did, in reality, print an exactly equivalent sum of new government-created money and yet in 2015 the UK has had zero per cent inflation.

To put this figure in context: total UK government debt in March 2010 was £759 billion and by March 2013, when the programme had ended, it was a gross sum of £1,185 billion.[2] So, over this period the government issued £426 billion of debt but during the same period the Bank of England – which is wholly owned by the UK government[3] – repurchased £375 billion of government debt from those who owned it.

It is important to say that the debt repurchased was not necessarily the debt issued and the price paid for the debt purchased (£375 billion) may not have been the same amount as it was issued for: that is because debt once issued is not always traded at its face value.[4]

53

However, give or take a bit, the fact is that most of the value of new UK government debt issued from 2009 until well into 2012 was effectively cancelled by the Bank of England simply creating money out of thin air to buy back a broadly similar amount of government debt in the financial markets.

This issue of creating money out of thin air is important and needs explanation because, as will become clear, it is intimately related to the way in which taxes also work. Most people think money is notes and coin, or at least something created by government in place of notes and coin, and of fixed amount. This, however, is now acknowledged not to be true by the Bank of England, although it took some time to get them to do so.[5] The reality that is now accepted to be true by the Bank of England is that all money is created by banks making loans.

This acknowledgement challenges another common perception: most people think that when they ask a bank for a loan the money to form that loan will be money paid into the bank by other customers. In other words, the bank acts as an intermediary between lenders and borrowers. What has now been established is that this is not the case. Instead what the bank does when making loans is a conjuring trick that creates new money. The economic reality is that no savings deposits at all are technically needed for a bank to make a loan, and because this fact is, as I will show in due course, heavily related to a proper understanding of tax, it does need to be properly understood.

When a bank agrees to give you a loan they make that loan by effectively opening two accounts for you. One is a current account (for ease, let's assume you haven't already got one). The other is a loan account. If you borrow £10,000 what they then do is mark your current account as having £10,000 in it. You're now free to spend that however you like. At the same time they also mark your loan account as having £10,000 in it. You now owe that to the bank. And if you add the two accounts together (one being a debit and the other a credit, or a plus and minus if you like) then they add up to nothing: if you decided to cancel the deal immediately after arranging the loan, you could straight away repay what you are shown as owing in the loan account by using the money you are shown as owning in the current account, and there would be nothing left.

Most importantly, please note that there's no cash involved in this process at all. It's just an accounting trick. Nothing more. Money is created by a stroke of a pen or some taps on a computer keyboard. There aren't any physical processes involved.

And also note that no one else's bank balance is involved or affected in any way as a result of this loan being created: the money lent to you did not belong to someone else before you got it: it was created afresh just for you as a result of you asking for a loan.

Of course that does not mean that other people will not be affected by this loan. Presumably you took it out to buy something. When you make that purchase you will pay the money from your current account and the recipient will pay it into their account. They will have more money (or reduce their overdraft) as a result. And this point is crucial: what this proves is that it is loans that create savings in an economy, and not the other way round – another statement the Bank of England now agrees is true.[6] And the same is true even if the recipient was in overdraft – in economic terms paying off an overdraft is identical in its impact to a person saving.

In Chapter 2 I demonstrated that most things people think about tax are wrong; it has to be said most things people think about money are wrong too. But at least, in the case of money, the Bank of England has now acknowledged some of the errors, and has even said that almost all the economics textbooks that describe banking are also wrong as a result.[7]

There are four further points to make about this process of money creation. The first is that there is, very clearly, profit to be made from creating money out of thin air. That's especially true when money is something that almost everybody wants, and which they are willing to pay to get their hands on, which is why banks can charge interest even though it cost them nothing to create the loan on which the interest is payable. No wonder banks are profitable.

Second, of course it is true that a bank can't repeat this lending trick for ever, because if it did people would eventually realize there was no substance behind the promise the bank makes when someone takes out a loan. That promise is that the loaned money now in the borrower's current account can be used to pay other people – a promise that is only as good as the bank on which the cheque is written. If a bank makes too many loans its ability to pay others may run out. Judging how much money can be lent before this point is reached is, of course, the confidence part of the trick of creating money.

The third is that, just as granting a loan creates money, repaying that loan destroys money. Loan repayment does not provide money for other people to borrow because that is not the process by which loans are made by banks; it simply takes the money that was lent out of circulation, for ever.

And lastly, since the government owns a bank – the Bank of England – it too can create money for its own use. Precisely because this is so easy, and partly also because commercial bankers wanted to protect their own right to create money, it is actually illegal for the Bank of England and other equivalent EU central banks to lend directly to the governments that own them, but this has been got round by quantitative easing.

In the quantitative easing process the government issues a debt (or gilt, as they are called) to a commercial bank which is then purchased by a Bank of England subsidiary company specially created for the purpose and to which the Bank of England has lent the money (made out of thin air) to pay for the debt. The net effect is that government debt ends up owned by the Bank of England, which is owned by the government, so that the debt is effectively cancelled because you can't owe yourself a debt. However, in the process of doing this money is created. Thus the government can indeed make money out of thin air as readily as any bank.

If you still doubt me (because this is important), let me try explaining it another way. Government bonds (or gilts) are loans from anyone in the private sector (but usually banks, pension funds and insurance companies) to the government. They are, then, government debt and private assets. Think of them as being a bit like a special form of bank deposit account with the government which does (as do all deposit accounts) pay interest but where, although you can't get your money back until a set time in the future (which could be thirty years away), you can instead sell some or all of your account to someone else. The Treasury bond or gilt is simply a chunk of this deposit account that can be sold. And in the case of quantitative easing it's the Bank of England that offers to buy this special type of deposit account from you – by buying your Treasury bond or gilt. If the price is right, and the Bank of England will make sure it is, you'd be daft not to sell your account to them – you make a profit by doing so. The net result is that you now have cash when you previously had a Treasury bond or gilt, whilst the Bank of England now owns the Treasury bond or gilt that you once owned – so it now owns the loan you made to the government. And all this was done with money that the Bank of England made specially for the purpose in exactly the same way that the £10,000 loan that I mentioned previously was created: it was all made out of thin air. So the net effect is that now the government owes money to the Bank of England, but because it owns the Bank of England it means, as I have said before, that the debt in question is effectively cancelled because you can't owe yourself money. In the meantime, whoever previously owned the Treasury bond or gilt now has freshly created money instead, made out of thin air, which they can now go and spend. Debt has been cancelled and money has been created and whilst, of course, all money is ultimately a government debt (which is why notes have the phrase 'I promise to pay the bearer' on them), it's also true they are never repaid and don't carry interest. The government debt that once carried interest can now be interest free. And the deficit that gave rise to the Treasury bond or gilt has now been replaced by newly created money, which just goes to prove that this is exactly what a government does when it runs a deficit – it creates government-made money.

If you don't believe this you wouldn't be alone. Indeed, the person who in my opinion was the second greatest economist of the last century, J. K. Galbraith, said:

> *The process by which banks create money is so simple that the mind is repelled.*[8]

He was right: the process is so simple that we're repelled by it. But now you know it's true, and the Bank of England said so in 2014. It's also true that the UK's quantitative easing funding has effectively cancelled government debt, as evidenced by the fact that the Bank of England now hands the interest paid to it by the Treasury as a result of it owning government debt straight back to the Treasury from whence it came. That debt therefore now costs the government virtually nothing[9] – and if that is not effectively debt cancellation it is hard to know what is.

So, there is proof that the government can print money to provide public services. It's just a matter of regret that politicians have not yet admitted the truth on this issue even though the Bank of England has been forced to do so.

The Office for Budget Responsibility, for instance, still states total national debt to include this cancelled sum,[10] which is profoundly misleading, at best. The fact that it is making such statements seems to be part of a whole political tactic of pretending that the government has run deficits of a scale that has simply not been true. That, in turn, appears to be part of the wider picture of not telling the truth about tax, whether deliberately or because the government genuinely does not understand it (a theme I will return to in the next chapter). Whichever is true, the reality is that from 2009 to 2012, despite what has been claimed by almost all politicians, the government did balance its books (near enough) without raising nearly enough tax to do so.

That leads us back to the question of why the government chooses to tax at all, when it would appear to be easier not to do so. The answer is that although in theory a government does not need to tax there are in practice some very good reasons why tax still makes sense, although, yet again, these reasons are not the ones usually heard.

First of all, the best, and in reality the main reason to use taxation is that tax lets a government reclaim the money it has spent into the economy, in order to stop the money supply over-expanding.

I have shown that both the government and the banks can create money out of thin air, and do so. In the case of commercial banks control is maintained by requiring that loans are repaid. That process of loan repayment, as noted above, quite literally destroys bank-created money. That's important: loan repayment stops the amount of money in the economy increasing without check, which would result in inflation.

It is just as necessary that the government has

available to it a means of destroying the money it can create and spend at will into the economy, and that mechanism is taxation. Taxation literally counterbalances government spending by reclaiming all or part of it from the economy. But what it never does is pay for the spending in the first place because any government can spend without tax. The almost universal commonplace that governments raise tax so that they can spend is a myth.

I stress the point, the spending always came first. It may, rather like the chicken and egg conundrum, be hard to tell that now, as the spend-and-tax cycles run seemingly side-by-side, but that was not always the case. Let's go centuries back in history where we can see that kings did not start by raising taxes and saving up a war chest, and only then decide who they were going to pick a fight with. They instead, all too often, picked the fight, raised an army, borrowed the money to pay the soldiers (because this was in the days before they owned their own banks), and then raised the tax to repay the loans. Central banks were in due course created to get rid of the commercial banks as middle-men in this process, but the fact remains that the spending has always come first, and the tax second. So tax cancels the money-creation process, and does not pay for the spend itself.

So, counter-intuitive as it may seem, tax is not about money-raising, as most people think. It does not have that function. It reclaims the money the government has already spent.

You may think this is a trivial distinction, that reclaiming money spent is effectively the same thing as raising money, but it isn't, by some way, and the change of perspective has some profound effects. First, consider the argument made in the previous chapter that all tax due does actually belong to the government. If you look on tax as reclaiming what the government has spent into the economy this makes total sense.

Secondly, if you think of tax as raising money, and therefore that government has to raise money in the first instance before it can then spend, you always, and automatically, presume that the capacity to spend is constrained by the amount of tax a government can raise, but, as I argue in this book, that is just not true. Because of the interaction between money and tax a government can always spend what it wants subject only to the constraints of inflation and the capacity of its economy to produce. Tax simply disappears as a constraint in that case, which should result in a radically altered mindset.

In addition, if you see the spending as the primary part of the tax-and-spend relationship (and it is) then the process of reclamation of the money expended has to be consistent with the goals of the spending – else why would you spend in the first place? If the spending is for social objectives, and much of it will be in the case of a modern government, then tax has to be designed with that fact in mind. Arguments about 'tax efficiency', to some extent at least, become secondary in tax system design when tax and spend are seen not as unrelated issues but as wholly integrated mechanisms that a government can use to achieve its goals. This will be a recurring theme of this book; it demands that we think about tax in a wholly new way.

It is important to note that the process of tax reclamation from the economy is not neutral. There are, in fact, five functions that tax can fulfil when it is seen as a cash reclamation process, all of which are about the government putting its economic policies into effect through its control of this money recovery exercise.

The first of these other reasons (and so reason no. 2 in the overall list) for raising tax is that, as the modern monetary theory school of economic thinking suggests, unless a government demands that taxes be paid using the currency that it issues there is no obvious reason for people to use that government-created currency in the economy it is trying to manage. In other words, the reason for demanding payment of tax is to make the local currency, issued, backed and controlled by the government, the only useful currency in that place.

The first time you come across this suggestion, which for many readers will be right now, it does seem a little odd. But the truth is, of course, that there are around the world many competing currencies that could be used for trading in any jurisdiction. Indeed, in countries where the shadow economy is very large, meaning that tax is rarely paid in full (if at all), there is ample evidence that currencies other than that issued by the local government are often used as the preferred basis for trading. This is why the US dollar is so popular in so many states where the shadow economy is significant in size.[11] It is also why so many wholly illegitimate activities – such as the drugs trade, where taxes are not, of course, paid – are also known to favour the dollar.

If, in contrast, those who trade know they will have to pay tax – whether it be VAT or income tax, national insurance and corporation tax – as a result of that trading, and know too that they can only settle that tax bill in the local currency of the country where they are trading, then they might as well remove all exchange risk from their transactions and actually use the local currency for the purposes of their trade in the first place. After all, such tax bills can (but won't always) amount to the single biggest combined outgoing of the business: to trade in any other currency makes no sense in that case. Modern monetary theorists suggest that governments know this, and have always done so. And that, they argue, is why official coinage was the required basis for the settlement of tax even in the pre-democratic era and is also why nothing much has, in this regard, changed since then.

The fact that government-issued coins and notes (or,

in the present day, currency in its various broader forms) are required for this purpose of paying tax also serves another purpose for the government issuing them. By creating a demand for its coins and notes to settle tax liabilities the state ensures that those same notes and coins become readily acceptable as payment for the goods and services the government itself wishes to buy within the economy it manages. The currency has a guaranteed value in exchange, which is the guarantee from the government that it will accept that currency back to settle debt: hence the 'promise to pay'. In turn this allows the government to do what it wants, which is to spend. The conclusion is quite extraordinary: the process of taxation ratifies the value of money, and in doing so has made the modern economy possible.

The second additional purpose for tax is to reorganize the economy to ensure that it delivers the government's economic goals.

Money is, of course, an issue of some importance in any economy. In fact, given that inflation was the sole issue of apparent concern in the mandate for the Bank of England from 1997 until recently, you might have gained the idea that money has been the *most* important issue to be addressed in the UK economy of late. I would strongly disagree: full employment, the sustainability of the economy and its ability to meet the real needs of those who live within it are all in my view of more importance than money; and yet if money is ignored none of those other objectives can be achieved.

The amount of money in an economy has a dramatic impact on the scale of economic activity that takes place within it, and just two factors – the relationship between the amount of tax the government collects and its total spending; and the amount of money that is created by the banks when making loans – determine how much money (or credit, because all money is a promise to pay) there is in that economy to facilitate the trades people want to undertake.

The process of controlling how much money there is in the economy, to ensure there is enough to allow people to make the transactions they want but without there being so much, or so little, that inflation or deflation results, is a key part of government economic management and underpins this third reason for tax.

The amount of commercial money creation is usually regulated by monetary policy, where the official base interest rate set by the Bank of England is the key economic variable. When this instrument of control fails – as it has over the last few years because banks have simply not been lending enough despite the base interest rate being near zero per cent – then the government has to control the economy through what is called fiscal policy instead.

When fiscal policy is used to manage the economy a government injects its own money into the economy to make good the shortfalls arising from insufficient commercial bank money creation: shortfalls that are effectively preventing the economy from running at full capacity (an issue explored in more depth in Chapter 4). There are two ways it can do this. The first is by running a deficit, i.e. spending more into the economy than it reclaims by tax, which then leaves money over in the economy, giving it a boost. The second is by quantitative easing.

Both these processes can, of course, be reversed: governments can run surpluses (as happened in the UK from 1998 to 2001), and bonds purchased via the quantitative easing process could be resold to the financial markets. That said, in the worldwide history of QE no bonds have been resold to date; and the running of surpluses is very rare. Deficit funding is the normal form of fiscal policy.

The purpose of both policies, monetary and fiscal, is to make sure that the economy keeps going when the markets do not deliver the outcome that a government desires within the economy that it manages. Almost invariably when fiscal policy is exercised – usually by deliberately setting tax revenues to be less than government spending – the desired outcome is an overall increase in economic activity and so an increase in GDP.

It is for good reason that fiscal policy is nearly always used in this one direction: there are very few governments on earth that would go through the aggravation of taxation at a higher level than its spending (so with no equivalent spending plans to justify it to the electorate), when it is instead much easier to control a booming economy by tightening bank lending conditions and raising interest rates, i.e. by using monetary policy, which is generally much less unpopular among voters.

This distaste for tax without spending is easily explained: since governments have no owners the idea of them accumulating money for its own sake makes no sense. Long-term government surpluses are, in fact, a logical absurdity for precisely that reason, especially when alternative measures to control market excess are available. They are just like imposing saving on the people of a country, and few electorates appreciate that happening to them. George Osborne might discover that if he ever really tries to run the long-term government surpluses he has said he plans to deliver. The infrequency of government surpluses over very long periods of history rather goes to prove the point.

And the reality is that there has never, to date, been a shortage of buyers for government debt either. Which Chancellor in that case wants to simultaneously incur the wrath of the electorate by imposing enforced saving on the country and the wrath of the financial markets by denying them the government debt they want to buy? No wise one would, I suggest, unless the need to control inflation made it absolutely essential, and that is a rare event in modern economies. This is precisely why fiscal policy is almost invariably about boosting the economy when activity falls short of desired levels whilst monetary policy is used to shrink it when markets get ahead of themselves, and government debt is, as a result, almost never repaid. This last point is not the big issue that politicians make of it either: the fact is that the owners of government debt think it's an asset and not a liability and most are happy to hold it for long periods of time and even pass it on to their children. To regard it as some sort of burden on future generations is therefore absurd: apart from anything else, as an asset it underpins many of the UK's pension funds which would be lost without it. Perhaps even more importantly, run surpluses until all government debt is repaid and you reach a point where there is no government-created money, at which time the economy would be at risk of outright collapse as the guarantee that underpins its medium of exchange would have gone. In that case, to be blunt, government surpluses can only ever be short-term exercises, at best.

To return to tax: governments clearly use taxation as an essential tool with which to reorganize the economy to achieve their desired outcomes. And precisely because governments are elected to manage the economy no one should really trust any politician who says that they have as their main goal the balancing of the government's books. Indeed that goal of a balanced budget makes no sense at all when read in the above context. It is, for example, possible in the right circumstances for the government to spend way in excess of the amount collected in tax and yet have no impact on inflation whilst delivering the completely beneficial effect of keeping the economy going when it would otherwise collapse from lack of demand, as the quantitative easing programme of 2009–12 demonstrated. The same is true of current government deficits, despite which we have no effective inflation in the UK.

In fact, what anyone who proposes that government must run a balanced budget is saying is that the government should not undertake the job of managing the economy for the benefit of the people who elect it, and that the economy should instead be allowed to run out of control if something goes wrong in the markets, with the government simply standing aside and letting that happen. In a modern democracy there is no way that such an attitude is consistent with what is expected by any electorate, and the policy of balancing a budget is, as a result, either recklessly irresponsible, or a completely false promise made by politicians which they will inevitably fail to deliver.

It is, I stress, no modern realization that this is the case. Abraham Lincoln told Congress:

> *The monetary needs of increasing numbers of people advancing towards higher standards of living can and should be met by the*

> *government. Such needs can be met by the issue of national currency and credit through the operation of a national banking system [or designated monetary authority]. The circulation of a medium of exchange issued and backed by the government can be properly regulated and redundancy of issue avoided by withdrawing from circulation such amounts as may be necessary by taxation, re-deposit and otherwise. Government has the power to regulate the currency and credit of the nation.*[12]

The interaction between money, inflation, the need to deliver economic activity for the benefit of all and the role that taxation has to play in that process has, then, long been appreciated. It has also, unfortunately, been long forgotten by some, at cost to us all.

Keeping the economy going forward is, however, for most governments, only one objective out of many. There are others where tax can also play a significant role. So, for example, since the Second World War most governments have, as a result of the universal suffrage that has had its greatest impact since then, made one of their key objectives the redistribution of income and wealth from those who can command considerable sums of one or both to those presently lacking sufficient to enjoy an adequate standard of living. The success, or otherwise, of these policies is something worthy of discussion, but not at this point; from the current perspective what is important is that most governments have not just paid lip service to this objective, but have also appeared to make some effort to achieve it. Given the disparities between words and action that I have noted so far with regard to tax this might be considered something of a surprise: a rare consistency between stated objectives and practice. None the less it is entirely appropriate to say that the redistribution of both income and wealth within an economy is the fourth reason for taxing.

That does not mean that taxation is the only way to achieve this goal: redistribution of income can, of course, be achieved through government spending. This happens when the government makes payments through a social security system to those in need. As already noted there is no reason for that spending to necessarily be financed by tax collected, and so it is possible for some redistribution to take place within an economy without tax being involved. It is fair to say, however, that most countries do deliberately use their tax systems to redistribute both income and wealth as a matter of policy.[13]

The fifth reason for taxing is also policy related. Most people realize that whilst markets, like taxation, are a remarkable human invention that has enormously increased the well-being of humankind they do, inevitably, sometimes get things wrong. This happens when the price a market sets for goods or services does not take into consideration all the costs or benefits that result from the trade in that activity.

A very obvious example is to be found in the case of oil. Our economy would simply not function without oil at the present time and yet we know that burning oil creates enormous side-effects that economists call externalities. The most obvious of these externalities from oil is pollution, which we do need to manage through repricing via the tax system; but there are two further side-effects, also obvious, that would never be reflected in the market price for oil unless a tax charge was added to it. The first of these is global warming; the second is the fact that oil is going to run out and therefore, long in advance of that happening, any responsible government needs to invest in alternative technologies that ensure society will continue to have the energy it needs after the time that the oil wells will have run dry. By adding tax to the price that we pay for oil-based products, most especially petrol and diesel, repricing reflects the policy intended to achieve these purposes.

There are, of course, other examples of externalities. For instance, tobacco and alcohol products carry additional charges that help fund the impact upon health services, and the cost of care for those who suffer the consequences of using these products.

Now, some will be cynical about this claim that such taxes are charged to reflect the externalities inherent in the products to which they relate. They will instead say that because the products in question are either essential or addictive they have what is called a very low price elasticity of demand, meaning that if tax is added to them, even in significant amount, the demand for the product remains largely intact and that this simply makes them a very easy way of raising tax. There is no question but that the price inelasticity of such products has been exploited in the past (as, for example, with the tax imposed on tea imported into the USA which gave rise to the Boston Tea Party and all that followed from it), but it is now likely that the correction of externalities not reflected in their prices is the main reason for taxing these items.

It is also possible to bring the price of an item down by tax-related means. This is often found in the case of VAT. Things like food, children's clothes, books, new homes, rents and other essential transactions are not subject to VAT in the UK precisely because the government wants to ensure that these goods and services are affordable, as a matter of policy. It uses tax (VAT in this case) to underprice them relative to other goods and services.

This fifth use for tax is, then, best described as repricing those goods and services where the government thinks that the market has failed to reflect social or external costs in the prices that would otherwise be set.

There is a sixth, and last, reason to tax. Chapter 1 explained how over the course of our history the relationship between tax and democracy is intimate, and to some extent inextricable. That remains the case today and there is some evidence (which I think compelling but about which not everyone will agree) that the more a person perceives a direct relationship between the tax they pay and the government, the more likely it then is that person will vote in elections. So, for example, in the UK many more people vote in general elections than other polls because, I suggest, income taxes are a matter of significance to many who vote and the role of income tax in the relationship between those many voters and the government is obvious. On the other hand, fewer people vote in local government elections because there are many who appreciate that the taxes that they pay to local government represent only a small part of its total spending and have, therefore, little impact on its decision-making process. The same could also be argued of European Union elections where there is no obvious tax connection at all.

It is consequently my belief that it is important that everyone does pay some income tax, and that is precisely why I have so much difficulty with the suggestion that taking people out of income tax (but no other tax) is beneficial. I do not think that is the case: I think that such a policy instead leaves people alienated from government and that this undermines the effectiveness of our democracy. I strongly suspect that, given the psychological importance accorded to income tax, this is another relationship that also works in reverse: over time governments come to think that people who do not pay that tax do not matter. The final reason for taxing is, then, to raise representation.

Taking all these factors together we have six reasons for any government to tax, all of which conveniently start with R:

1. Reclaiming money the government has spent into the economy for re-use
2. Ratifying the value of money
3. Reorganizing the economy
4. Redistributing income and wealth
5. Repricing goods and services
6. Raising representation

With that range of reasons for taxing it is not surprising that it remains high on most governments' agendas. It is clear tax really does deserve its role at the heart of economic debate. All that remains to be said is it's a shame that so much nonsense is talked about it. Correcting that nonsense is the subject of later chapters.

4

Dealing with the naysayers

Tax, as the first three chapters of this book have shown, is not something most of us need to be compelled to pay. As even HM Revenue & Customs say, the reality is that most of us pay tax voluntarily.

And as those same chapters note, the idea that tax is about raising money to pay for the government's spending is wrong. Any government can spend without taxing, if it so wishes, although for the very good reasons noted in Chapter 3, few would want to do without taxation altogether. That's because most politicians realize that tax is very often the most effective way in which a government can influence the working of the economy for which it is responsible for the benefit of the people it has been charged with governing.

It is for precisely this reason that tax is not about oppression, a loss of freedom or even a loss of income;

it's actually about how to make collective choices that work best for the communities we all live in. That is why most of us pay it. We know from our own experience that tax does help deliver to us things that we quite definitely want, and would now find very difficult to do without, and on which we want a say, which democracy allows.

The truth is that debate about tax should be all about choice, and most of the rest of this book will have that subject as its recurring theme. But before getting to that discussion it is vital to note that there are some who would really rather that we talked about other things when it comes to tax. Their arguments have to be addressed head on before we can consider the great things tax can do for us.

There are, broadly speaking, three groups who wish to undermine tax debate, all of whose voices are heard very loudly whenever the subject is raised at present.

One group is, by and large, made up of mainstream politicians. For entirely erroneous reasons, which I in part explored in Chapter 3 and will now explore in more depth below, they now appear to suffer from selective ignorance when it comes to taxation. As a consequence almost all politicians are offering a prescription of austerity as a solution to all economic ailments. This, I think, is bizarre, because for reasons that I will explain such a policy cannot work to achieve their stated objective of a balanced budget, despite which almost all seem committed to the famous Thatcher mantra that 'there is no alternative'. As a result they are collectively denying us the Joy of Tax, for reasons that I suspect most of them do not understand.

Another group, in contrast, do in my opinion know exactly what they're doing when it comes to tax. These people are libertarians based in think tanks such as the Institute of Economic Affairs, the Taxpayers' Alliance and bodies such as the Institute of Directors. Their object is, in the apparent name of freedom, to deny us the Joy of Tax by making sure that democratic choice with regard to tax, as most would understand it, is not available in the future. They hope to deliver this under the guise of flat taxes, whose false allure is something I will address in this chapter.

Lastly, there are people who really do not want tax to work as it should. On the whole these people are motivated by what can best be described as greed, although they do their utmost to hide it. Indeed, many of them do their utmost to hide everything they do because they are undermining the effective operation of the existing tax system so that it cannot deliver what is intended of it. Much of that opposition activity is located in tax havens where the people doing the dirty work are very often accountants, lawyers and bankers, whose clients are the largest companies and some of the wealthiest people in the world. There are also those who cheat the system more locally by evading more mundane taxes; all are seeking to undermine the collective objectives that the tax system strives to fulfil.

Given the strength of these three lobbies it is no wonder that it has been hard to see how tax can do its best for us. We need to examine how and why so many powerful, and sometimes misguided, interests have been lined up against it before we can turn, in the following chapters, to look at the choices we could make with regard to tax if only these objections are overcome. The objections each of the three groups raise will be considered in turn, starting with the dogmatic ideology of libertarian flat tax proponents.

The deniers of choice

There are in the UK some who really do want to deny us choice with regard to tax, and they know exactly what they are doing. To put it bluntly, what they're up to is not subtle: their aim is to ensure that the choices that tax enables (as noted in the previous chapter) are taken off the political agenda for good – and in the process it seems pretty clear that they want to undermine democracy itself.

These people are right-wing libertarians. They are well funded and populate many think tanks located around Westminster of which the best known are probably the Institute of Economic Affairs (often referred to as 'Margaret Thatcher's favourite think tank', with some justification), the Adam Smith Institute (whose name-sake would likely shudder at much of what they say) and the so-called Taxpayers' Alliance, whose relation-ship with most taxpayers seems remote at best. All of them are secretive about their funding. None make it clear in whose interests they really act, but what they do undoubtedly have in common are a number of beliefs that most of us would find pretty odd, and in some cases quite alarming.

Some of these organizations have a strange relation-ship with democracy. As an example, in 2005 the Institute of Economic Affairs published a paper by Brad Walmsley under the title 'The Corruption of Universal Suffrage: Tax, consent and the tyranny of the majority'.[1] In it he argued that:

> *Simple majority rule results in a tyranny of the*
> *majority. Politicians auction taxes in order to*
> *buy votes, oppressing the productive and*
> *producing economic instability. But simple*
> *majority rule is inferior to the historic right to*
> *just government. Since taxpayers cannot be said*
> *to have consented to taxation under simple*
> *majority rule, it represents unjust government.*
> *Therefore, the power to tax must be separated*
> *from the legislature since it is elected by*
> *universal suffrage. Consent to taxation can only*
> *be obtained from the taxpayers casting one vote*

> *for every pound of tax they pay; you have more*
> *say, the more you pay.*

This is an idea about as far removed from the concept of democracy as it is possible to get. It is really an argument for plutocracy, a system of government where those ruling are granted power by virtue of their wealth.

The fact that Walmsley also argues that people have not consented to tax by voting in elections might surprise many: this idea is very obviously untrue, but the argument is made time and again by those organizations. So, in 2014 Tim Worstall, an Adam Smith Institute fellow, stated that 'democracy is not all it's cracked up to be'[2] whilst in 2012 Adam Smith Institute director Dr Eamonn Butler wrote about the 'tyranny of the majority'[3] – a term much favoured by these groups. What they mean by it is that the right that democracy on the basis of universal suffrage provides to a government to create progressive taxation is an assault by the majority on the rights of the wealthy minority.

The ethos of these groups is, in fact, very clear. They focus upon the individual, the rights of private property, the primacy of markets and the abuse that they think flows from the ability of democratically elected government to interfere in these rights (which they consider inalienable) in the collective best interest, which they do not recognize exists. They seek to promote their viewpoint in a number of ways. The method most relevant to the discussion here is their promotion of what they call flat taxation.

Those who propose flat taxes promote them by saying that they are 'simple' and that as we would all like tax to be simple this must mean flat taxes are good for us. Nothing could be further from the truth for most people in this country, so let me clarify what most flat tax proposals involve.

First of all they always focus upon income tax even though, as I noted in Chapter 2, that tax represents only about 27 per cent of all UK tax revenues at present. With regard to this tax it is always suggested that there should be a single tax rate, with all higher rates of tax being abolished as a result. So, for example, the latest serious proposal for a flat tax in the UK, which has come from something called the 2020 Tax Commission, a joint venture between the Taxpayers' Alliance and the Institute of Directors,[4] suggests a flat tax rate of 30 per cent. In this particular proposal that would cover national insurance charges as well as income tax, which would mean that, while many people currently paying basic rate tax would find their overall tax rate falling a little, many pensioners and those who live on modest investment incomes would see a significant increase in their overall tax rate since at present they do not pay national insurance.

This flat income tax would include a single personal

allowance, which this so-called Commission suggests should be set at £10,000 a year, although that is now less than is already available under the existing income tax law in the UK. On the grounds that this personal allowance would ensure that those on low incomes would always pay slightly less in tax as a proportion of income than those on higher incomes, flat tax proponents argue that their tax proposals are progressive, but that is, as is so commonly the case in taxation, a claim that involves some misrepresentation of the truth.

The first misrepresentation is that whilst flat tax proponents argue that they will simplify the tax system by abolishing a number of allowances and reliefs, including for example those on pension contributions, they also always seemingly wish to open some enormous loopholes that could only ever be of real benefit to those with significant income. So they would, for example, not only abolish all higher rates of tax but would also abolish all taxes on company profits, stamp duty, inheritance tax and all taxes on capital gains.

Such proposals are not put forward by chance or with the aim of tax simplification. It is, of course, the case that higher rates of income tax, the highest rates of stamp duty and almost all capital gains tax and inheritance tax are paid by the well-off minority whose wealth these organizations seek to protect. These taxes and rates do, after all, represent 'the tyranny of the majority' in the opinion of those who propose flat taxes.

What those proponents of flat taxes usually fail to mention, however, is that abolishing all these taxes and replacing them with flat taxes would also provide those possessing wealth with considerable opportunity to avoid the remaining flat income tax. So, for example, if an individual transferred their employment income to a company and did not subsequently withdraw it by way of salary or dividend, then under flat tax proposals that income would go completely untaxed for as long as it remained within the company, which could be for an indefinite period. The ability to make ends meet without having to rely upon one's earnings is, of course, something that only a few can enjoy, and, by definition, those people are wealthy. Flat taxes would, therefore, let those who are already wealthy accumulate their earnings tax-free, in a way denied to everyone else. That is the complete antithesis of a progressive tax system.

In that case the so-called simplicity of flat taxes actually encourages and permits tax avoidance by a wealthy few, while making sure that most of the rest pay any tax they owe. The result would be that flat taxes would considerably increase inequality of wealth and of after-tax income. Almost all research now shows both those inequalities to be profoundly harmful to the health of any society, as even the World Economic Forum (hardly a den of left-wing thinking) has now recognized.[5]

This is an outcome that the think tanks promoting flat taxes seldom seem to mention.

Another odd feature of flat taxes rarely mentioned by their proponents when they claim that everyone will benefit from them is that VAT and other so-called indirect taxes – alcohol and tobacco duties, fuel duties and the like – all seem to be ignored by these proposed reforms, and yet it is these taxes that hit many of the people with lowest incomes in this country hardest of all, whereas income taxes have little impact on them at present. This is confirmed by the Office for National Statistics. In 2011–12, which is the year for which information is most recently available at the time of writing,[6] households with the lowest 20 per cent of incomes in the UK paid just 10.2 per cent of their total incomes in direct taxes like income tax (to which flat tax reforms would apply) and 26.5 per cent of their income in indirect taxes such as VAT (to which flat tax reforms would not apply), whereas households in the top 20 per cent of income earners paid 24.7 per cent of their total incomes in direct taxes and only 10.8 per cent in indirect taxes. Leaving aside the important point that as a result the bottom 20 per cent of income earners actually paid a higher proportion of their income in tax than the top 20 per cent (36.7 per cent compared to 35.5 per cent) under the present system, it is evident that flat tax reforms, by addressing only direct taxes, would leave those on lower incomes largely where they are now in the amount of tax they pay, while delivering big tax cuts for those on higher incomes. As a result, and yet again, inequality would increase.

No one should, then, be in any doubt that proposals for flat taxes are all about big tax cuts for those who are already well off and about little or no change at all, at least in tax rates, for those on lower incomes. This is hardly surprising, because this is exactly what the political philosophy of those proposing these taxes would lead one to expect.

This, however, is not the end of the story. If large tax cuts are proposed for the well off and a whole raft of other taxes are to be abolished, then there is another inevitable consequence to be considered: if inflation is to be avoided, government spending must fall to match the reduced amount that the state can recover from the economy by way of tax. The 2020 Tax Commission makes a virtue of this, saying that in their view no more than 33 per cent of national income should be taken by way of tax as government revenue. In fact it sets this as both a target and a cap. In doing so, they do, of course, make the mistake noted in Chapter 3 of thinking that tax is raised to cover spending and not to reclaim what has already been spent, but this error may be deliberate on their part because the proposal is specifically intended to cap spending.

Again, there should be no surprise about this: all the organizations promoting flat taxes believe that the state

Figure 3: UK government spending as a percentage of GDP, 1900–2010

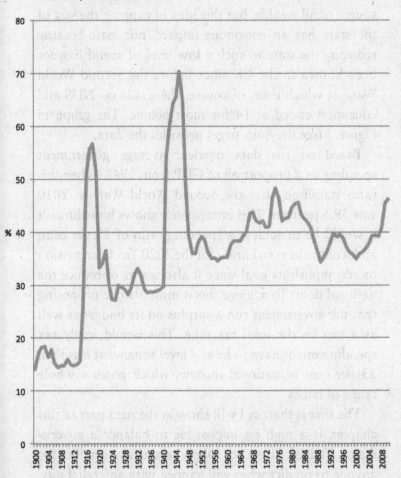

Source: UKPublicSpending.co.uk

is inefficient, that its role in the economy should be kept as small as possible and that the private sector is the source of all wealth. But this idea of capping the size of the state has an enormous impact, not least because reducing the state to such a low level of spend has not been known in the UK since before the Second World War,[7] at which time, of course, there was no NHS and education ended at 14 for most people. The graph in Figure 3 (see previous page) provides the data.

Based on the data overleaf average government spending as a proportion of GDP from 1948 (when this ratio stabilized after the Second World War) to 2010 was 39.5 per cent. This immediately shows how difficult it would be to achieve a spending ratio of 33 per cent; and it might be even harder for the 2020 Tax Commission to accomplish its goal since it also wants to reduce the national debt. To achieve this it must also be proposing that the government run a surplus on its budget as well as a cap on the total tax take. This would imply tax spending might have to be at a level somewhat less than 33 per cent of national income, which poses a whole range of issues.

The first is that, as I will show in the next part of this chapter, it is nigh on impossible to balance a government's budget. There are simply too many variables for anyone to predict what will happen with any reliability. Despite what politicians like to say it seems that people inherently realize this. So, when Alistair Darling tried to decree by Act of Parliament[8] in 2010 that there would be a steady decline in the government deficit over the life of the next parliament, no one believed him. It seems as likely that no one will believe George Osborne's plans to mandate government surpluses, announced in 2015. The reason was succinctly explained by George Osborne himself in the House of Commons in 2010:

> *Let us remember what one of the economists whom the Prime Minister himself appointed to the Monetary Policy Committee has said about the Bill. Willem Buiter has said: 'Fiscal responsibility acts are instruments of the fiscally irresponsible to con the public.'*[9]

Likewise no one should believe flat tax proponents when they say that they can achieve the same outcome. The fact is that a government has sometimes, as it did in 2008, to pick up the pieces when things go wrong in the economy.

The flat tax proponents' commitment to cap government income and spending is, in that case, a deliberate attempt on their part to stop the government intervening in the economy for the public good, come what may. This would effectively remove the management of the economy from the remit of government, wholly undermining much of the purpose for taxation as noted in the previous chapter. When coupled with the move to end redistribution via tax, through the removal of so many taxes on those from whom wealth would otherwise be redistributed, and the effective elimination of taxes that might be used to reprice market failures, flat taxes can be seen as a coordinated effort to close off many of the options that a government has to use tax for social purposes. This, then, would severely curtail the scope for action of any democratic government – because the cap on revenue and spending is deliberately designed to reduce the choices available in a democracy and is as such a direct assault upon democracy itself.

This is not by chance. In 2006 I interviewed Alvin Rabushka, the co-creator of the flat tax idea.[10] He told me then:

> *I think we should go back to first principles and causes and ask what government should be doing and the answer is 'not a whole lot'. It certainly does way too much and we could certainly get rid of a lot of it. We shouldn't give people free money. You know, we should get rid of welfare programmes, we need to have purely private pensions and get rid of state-sponsored pensions. We need private schools and private hospitals and private roads and private mail delivery and private transportation and private everything else. You know government shouldn't be doing any of that stuff. And if it didn't do any of that stuff it wouldn't need all of that tax money so that's the*

fundamental position and as long as you're going to have government do all that stuff you're going to have all those high taxes.[11]

This is democratic choice under attack in its most extreme form. Few flat tax advocates would go as far as Rabushka, but you need to see what he says to realize where those who propose these taxes are coming from. It's not an exaggeration to say that their agenda is to take away your right to choose.

We should also be under no illusion about the fact that this would be at enormous cost to us all. In 2008 when the banks nearly collapsed, a flat tax system with a cap on government spending would have meant the government could not have intervened to save the economy. It would have gone to the wall, and with it most business in this country as well as the savings of a great many households. Unemployment would have increased more rapidly than it did, and there would have been no capacity to pay any compensation to those thrown out of work through no fault of their own. And as GDP would, inevitably, have fallen, the situation would have got worse, since a cap fixed as a ratio of GDP requires that spending falls in recession – which would exacerbate the impact of failings in the market economy and create more extreme boom and busts, which is exactly what most people would think government should work to prevent but which flat taxation makes considerably more likely.

Figure 4: Government receipts and spending as a percentage of GDP, 1997–2014

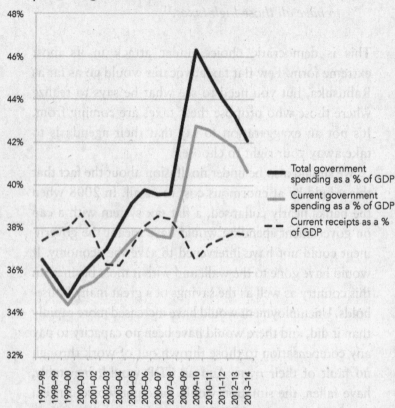

Source: Author's calculations based on HM Treasury budget data over the period

In that case it is vital to realize that flat taxes are not really about just having one rate of income tax or about tax simplification. They're about limiting the power of democracy and letting markets run riot without any ability to constrain the consequences. That, I suspect, is not what many of those who find flat taxes superficially attractive on the basis of their so-called ability to simplify the tax system might want but, as seems to be so commonplace with regard to tax, what is said about flat taxes and what is actually the case are almost the opposite of each other.

The veil of ignorance

The crash of 2008 had enormous consequences for our economy, and will continue to do so for a long time to come. One reason for that is the amount of nonsense that has been spoken by so many politicians from so many parties on the way to tackle these issues, especially since 2010. From that year onwards most politicians in most countries impacted by the crash of 2008 have seemed to think that the biggest problem they face is the size of their government's deficit. In thinking this they reflect the idea that tax is raised to allow spending, and not, as is actually the case, that tax is the reclamation of spending that has already happened.

It's important to be clear about the UK government deficit. The UK government's spending and income from 1997 to 2014, expressed as a proportion of national income, is shown in Figure 4 (see opposite page). Government income during this period remained very near the long-term normal rate of around 38 per cent of

GDP. Spending patterns, on the other hand, varied significantly. From 1997 until 2002 government income exceeded all its spending, whether on current commitments (like paying staff in the NHS) or on investment (such as building new hospitals).

As will also be noted, if one excludes expenditure on investment, government income overall exceeded spending until 2007–8. It was only the decision by the government to invest more heavily after 2002 that resulted in total government spending exceeding income; and it is perfectly normal practice to borrow in order to invest (or to spend ahead of recovering money from the economy in the case of a government). Also note that whilst there was borrowing, the sums involved were fairly small, commonly little more than 1 to 2 per cent of GDP.

I make these observations for what should be a very obvious reason, which is that spending appeared to almost everybody to be well and truly under control until 2008. That 'almost everybody' included David Cameron and George Osborne, who were during this period committing themselves to matching Labour spending plans.

It is also evident from these data that in the period when the economy was overheating, from 1997 to 2001, the government reorganized the economy by effectively withdrawing money from it through deliberate underspending: fiscal policy to constrain an over-exuberant market was in operation. In the aftermath of the dot.

com crash, when the government feared that a recession was possible, it again intervened to reorganize the economy for the benefit of people of this country: this time by investing, deliberately overspending in order to inject money into the economy (and build a lot of schools and hospitals in the process). The aim was to prevent a downturn in the wake of a serious stock market crash where the FTSE 100 halved in value (which is a fact often forgotten), and the policy was successful, according to the criteria that all politicians had agreed upon: growth continued uninterrupted and people rewarded the Labour government by re-electing it. This was tax at work in the way democracy intended.

It was in 2008 that everything changed. Government income fell because the economy went into recession. Some big companies went into a period of heavy loss-making and a lot of people lost their jobs. Those companies and those people stopped paying corporation tax and income tax as a result. More significantly, expenditure by government had to increase. Part of that was automatic: if more people are unemployed and the incomes of those who are employed are falling in real terms, as they have been for most people in the UK since 2009,[12] then it is inevitable that government spending on both in-work and unemployed social security benefits will increase.

There is another point to note though: in 2009 the then Labour government substantially increased its investment in the UK economy with the deliberate aim (as in 2002) of averting a serious economic crisis. This worked: the evidence appears unambiguous. By 2010 the UK economy was recovering because of the money that the UK government had injected into it. But then investment by the new government was cut, as Figure 4 shows: much less money was spent into the economy whilst the amount recovered from it remained broadly consistent, and there was a downturn again as a result. Unfortunately it remains the case at the time of writing that, in terms of per capita GDP, the UK is still a long way short of getting out of this situation.

Despite this, politicians of most of the UK's leading parties (the SNP, Greens and Plaid Cymru apart) remain dedicated to programmes of austerity under which they would all plan to cut government spending still further between 2015 and 2020. This, they argue, will ensure that the UK government deficit is cleared. However, at the same time they all want to promise growth in UK GDP, which has, for better or worse, become the barometer of UK national economic competence.

Unfortunately, this combined goal of balancing the government's books while maintaining growth is for all practical purposes impossible to achieve. None the less these politicians continue to make the offer. I can think of three possible reasons for this, all worryingly unattractive.

First, the politicians involved might be knowingly

offering something they are aware is impossible to deliver. I trust that's not true because I retain the hope that politicians aim to tell the truth, although I am conscious that a great many people have given up on that expectation.

Alternatively, they may have been influenced by the dogma of the right-wing think tanks that this chapter has already explored, and as a result believe that it is their duty to cut the size and role of the government they want to be a part of, to fit what they believe to be the available tax revenues – when such a concept is meaning-less, as I argued in Chapter 3. If so, they have sold out on the democratic process, and that would, of course, justify the cynicism that many feel about their motives.

Thirdly, there is the possibility that they simply do not understand what they are offering and what the real nature of tax is. I am going to be generous and assume that in many cases this may be true; I therefore need to explain the real situation.

The first thing all politicians have to realize is that, as I have already shown, tax and money are pretty intimately related at a macroeconomic level. (Macro-economics is the process of looking at the economy as a whole.) In that case you would think that money and its relationship to tax would be a really important part of the study of macroeconomics, but it is not. Instead the subject is either very largely ignored or is incorrectly taught, as (with regard to money) the Bank of England had to admit in 2014. I did, of course, explore this issue in depth in Chapter 3, but because of the significance of the matter it is worth repeating some of the comment made in the Bank of England first Quarterly Bulletin for 2014, when it had to say things like:

> *the relationship between monetary policy and money differs from the description in many introductory textbooks*[13]

and

> *The reality of how money is created today differs from the description found in some economics textbooks*[14]

and

> *This article explains how, rather than banks lending out deposits that are placed with them, the act of lending creates deposits – the reverse of the sequence typically described in textbooks.*[15]

The Bank had to be blunt: what it was saying was that what had been taught to generations of economists about how money works was not just wrong but exactly the opposite of the truth.

Unfortunately, instead of this fact being recognized we still have to endure a prevailing political view of both money and tax that is based on misconceptions and so is crippling us. This incorrect view is essentially a micro-economic one that assumes that government works very much like a business. You will be familiar with this idea: many politicians refer to 'UK plc' as if the government operates like a quoted company.

The origin of the idea isn't hard to find: Margaret Thatcher very clearly based most of her economic under-standing on the corner shop run by her father. In this quite literally small world view of national economics the rule of Mr Micawber applies:[16] if money coming in from tax revenues exceeds money going out then every-thing will be just fine. If the reverse is true it is said misery results.

It is fair to say that this might have been true for Mr Micawber and it might well be true for a small business without an overdraft facility from a bank, but for a government this is complete nonsense, for one very obvious reason. This is that, unlike Mr Micawber and any business, a government with its own sovereign currency can, as explained in Chapter 3, print its own money whenever it wishes to make good a shortfall in its income. If, therefore, there are willing buyers for its debt (and this has been the uninterrupted case in the UK since 1694[17]), running a deficit (or reclaiming less tax from the economy than you spend) is simply not a problem for a government. You would think that missing this fact would be a cardinal sin for any economist, let alone politician, and yet it is the norm. Of course this situation of being able to run deficits would change if a time came when a government could not sell its debt, but, given that there is a savings glut in the world at present and a shortage of secure assets in which to invest, the prospect of the government being unable to sell its debt seems very unlikely for a long time to come.

So, it seems that the glaringly obvious has to be spelled out once again: there is no reason why any government should have to balance its books unless it really wants to do so as a matter of policy – which would only be wise if that economy was booming (as it was, for example, in the period 1997 to 2001), and the government wanted as a result to temporarily withdraw cash from the economy by underspending, and thus calm down over-activity to prevent an unsustainable boom. Since we are in nothing like that situation now, a balanced budget would be absurd. Indeed, it is very obvious that over-spending is essential at present if the economy is to get the cash it needs to keep going. And there is sound economic rationale behind this requirement for more cash to be injected, by effectively under-collecting tax, if the economy is not going to crash.

There are actually only four sectors in an economy at a macroeconomic level: national income is made up of total consumer spending plus total government spending plus total investment made in the economy plus total exports less the total cost of imports. Those are the only sectors that we need to consider. It is important to note that money and tax do not seem to be part of this equation. That's not by chance: this equation is about what really happens in the economy and not how we pay for it. However, there is a way in which money plays a very real part in this equation, since the four sectors trade with each other through the medium of the national currency; and, because of a simple accounting rule that for every debit there must be a credit, the interactions between them have to balance out. It is impossible for it to be otherwise.

Now if you combine the politicians' desire for GDP to rise, meaning that the sum of consumer spending, net investment, government spending and net exports must increase, with the necessity for transactions between the sectors to balance, something rather interesting happens which relates directly to the discussion on government spending and tax, and so to the scale of the deficit and the level of savings in an economy.

What the requirement of balance between the sectors demands is that if one sector borrows another must save, and vice versa. There is no alternative option: double-entry accounting requires that this is so. Thus if consumers save then someone else, whether it be the government, investors or the net overseas sector, must borrow. The overseas sector effectively borrows by net exporting, by the way; the corollary is that net importing represents saving in the UK, the saving being the amount by which we have not paid those in other countries for the net goods and services that we import, because they have effectively left the funds they are owed in sterling in the UK.

This is important. At present consumers are saving,[18] even if only by repaying their mortgages while interest rates remain low. Business is not investing:[19] indeed big business is sitting on record piles of cash.[20] And we are running a large and growing trade deficit,[21] meaning that the overseas sector is saving in the UK. There is only one net possible outcome of all this, and that is that the government has to borrow. It genuinely has no other option: the other sectors' behaviour have made that a necessity and there is nothing whatsoever, as the backer of the currency (which it is), that it can do about it.

To put this another way, politicians might say they can cut their way to closing the deficit, but that's just not true unless they want to crash the economy in the attempt to do so. What they seemingly fail to appreciate is that cutting spending to save cash and so reduce borrowing may be possible in a company but it's not in an economy. That's because in a company if, for example, you sack an employee they do, as far as the company is concerned, go away. In the case of the economy as a whole the situation is quite different. You can put a government employee out of work and if they cannot find another job – which

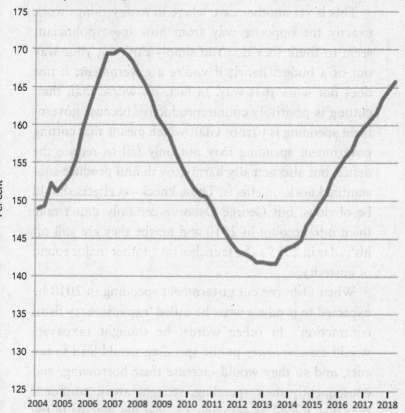

Figure 5: Household gross debt to income expressed as a percentage

Source: Office for Budget Responsibility Fiscal Forecasts, March 2014, Table 3.33[24]

is often what happens in a recessionary environment – they are still there in the country: they still need to be fed, educated and have health care, use the roads, claim benefits and be housed. Only now they aren't doing anything in exchange for all those needs being met.

This is yet another case where in reality things work exactly the opposite way from how most politicians seem to think they do. You simply can't cut your way out of a budget deficit if you're a government; it just does not work that way. In fact, it's worse than that: cutting is positively counterproductive because government spending is part of GDP, which means that cutting government spending may not only fail to reduce the deficit but also actually harm growth and produce substantial knock-on effects. Those knock-on effects should be obvious, but George Osborne certainly didn't take them into account in 2010 and maybe they are still off his radar in 2015 as he launches on another major round of austerity.

When Osborne cut government spending in 2010 he expected to produce what he called 'expansionary fiscal contraction'. In other words, he thought taxpayers would assume lower public spending would lead to tax cuts, and so they would increase their borrowing, and consequently their spending, straight away, confident that they would be enjoying a higher net income in the future. In that case, Osborne thought, the economy would expand as a result of his reducing the fiscal stimulus. It might sound bizarre, but that's the logic on which the economics of austerity was based.

But George Osborne was wrong. That's not what

Figure 6: Business investment as a percentage of GDP

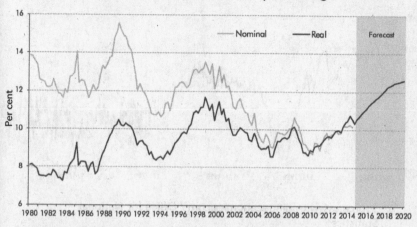

Source: Office for National Statistics, Office for Budget Responsibility[25]

people did. The UK's household savings ratio increased from an average of about 3 per cent of income from 2004 to early 2008 to an average of about 6 per cent from 2009 to 2014.[22] When matched with falling household incomes since 2009[23] this has meant that, overall, consumers have been spending less. The expansionary fiscal contraction George Osborne hoped for did not happen among consumers because they actually concluded that if all the safety nets that they were used to were being withdrawn as a result of reduced government spending, and the job security they hoped for was being reduced for the same reason, then they would need to save more for the proverbial rainy day. That was the

Figure 7: UK balance of trade from 1979

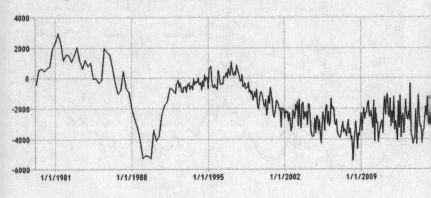

Source: www.tradingeconomics.com / Office for National Statistics[27]

obviously predictable reaction to government spending cuts, but was one George Osborne completely missed.

The graph in Figure 5 (see p. 105) illustrates how this played out in practice; it shows data from the Office for Budget Responsibility for actual changes in the ratio of household debt to household income in the UK from 2004 to 2014 and forecast changes on to 2019. Over the period for which the OBR then had data people were reducing their overall debt, which is the same as saving. But what the OBR forecast in 2014, and forecast again in 2015, is that there would be a change in the ratio with debt rising again thereafter.

I stress, they had no choice but to make this forecast: the OBR know all about the balances I am discussing here and know that if the government is to clear its deficit then someone else has to borrow, so they forecast that consumers would begin to do just that: it was the only way the OBR could say that government borrowing would be reduced.

They did the same with investment. Figure 6 (see p. 107) shows the Office for Budget Responsibility data on that, as at March 2015. In nominal and real terms business investment has been low, and is only just improving now, but what is clear is that to make the forecast of government debt reductions work the OBR is having to suggest that business investment will over the next few years reach all-time record highs, and that means companies will have to borrow. I hate to disillusion them, but there is not a hint that this is really going to happen.

Just for the record, Figure 7 (see opposite page) shows the balance of trade data from 1979 on. It's not too optimistic either, and with it being clear that emerging markets are unlikely to grow significantly in coming years as Chinese expansion slows, a dramatic change in our balance of trade is unlikely.[26]

Bringing all this together it's clear that in view of these trends – increasing private saving, which suppresses consumption and so GDP, and falling business investment, which also suppresses GDP, and broadly static trade – it has only been the government's overspending and its quantitative easing programme that have kept the economy going for the last few years.

What is also clear is that when the government says it will balance the budget it actually knows it can only do this if consumers and businesses (and households buying new houses, which counts as investment) spend a great deal more over the next few years than they have of late, and that they must borrow to do this. The price of falling government borrowing will, then, be substantial increases in private debt. If that does not happen then those cuts in government spending can only have one net outcome, and that will be a fall in GDP that will trigger more saving, less investment and maybe fewer exports as we lose whatever competitive edge we have, all of which are very bad news. These are the only two options available as a result of the chosen austerity policies of all major UK political parties (the SNP, Greens and Plaid Cymru excepted): either there is a private sector credit boom or we get seriously worse off and our economic security falls.

And all that is because politicians say they want to balance the government's books by making tax income equal the amount the government spends into the economy each year when, as I have shown, there is no reason for them to do that at all.

So why do they claim they must balance the books? Is it because they actively want a private credit boom (with the inevitable crash that will follow)? Or is it because they so dislike what the state does for people that they want to cut it come what may (the Conservative Party plans to cut state spending as a percentage of GDP from 41 per cent to 35 per cent during the 2015–20 parliament[28])? Are they hiding the truth, which is that if the government wants to run a surplus (i.e. it wants to spend less than it receives, which is a precondition of reducing debt) then someone else in this 'balancing act' has to run a deficit if GDP is to be near enough stable? Or is it that they just don't know?

This is not, I stress, to say that change is not possible. Given that the government's target to spend less cannot be achieved in isolation, as I have just shown, then alternatively consumers can be encouraged to spend more; but we must be clear about the consequences for debt in this case unless there is a policy to increase real wages. It's also possible to invest more and we could even try to run a trade surplus if we really wanted to balance the government's books, but the point about all three is that none of them can ever be achieved by cuts in government spending: that's impossible. These things can only happen if, for example, the government gives a sound reason to business or consumers to spend more – and its rhetoric on cuts in spending and jobs does just the opp-osite of that (because the government is both the biggest spender and the most significant employer in the country). Or to put it another way, the pursuit of austerity actually guarantees that the government will fail in its objective of balancing its books. Which means that if we are to clear the government's deficit the only way to do it in the current environment is for the government to spend.

Yes, you read that right. The truth is that the government has to spend if it wants to save. Because if it spends it creates jobs. If it creates jobs it has more people paying tax and fewer on social security benefits. And if the increase in number of jobs creates an increased demand for workers, employees' real wages rise. And that further increases the government's tax take and also reduces in-work benefits. And of course that in turn leads to more consumer spending, and so more tax take. And then business invests to meet consumer demand and so GDP rises, and tax take with it. And on, and on, in a virtuous circle that ensures that the deficit falls (which calms overseas investors' nerves). And when GDP rises and tax take increases the government can cut its own spending or withdraw more from the economy in tax and that does not harm GDP, while the increased revenue take ensures that the government heads towards a balanced budget.

And what's more, people are very obviously happier. And that's the Joy of Tax. It simply works to deliver well-being when nothing else can. All we need to do is have enough people tell politicians that this is truly how it is. I nominate you for the job; I am already on the case.

Those who don't want to make tax work

What this chapter has so far shown is that we have some people who deny us choice with regard to tax because they do not realize how it really should work, and others who would deliberately deny us the choices that tax makes available if only they could. That just leaves to be considered those who really don't want the tax system to work as it should for reasons of their own self-interest.

In very many ways the story of this group of people needs less telling than do those of the first two, precisely because most people have already heard of this group. Those who do not want the tax system to work as it should are called tax abusers, although it should be said they come in two distinct varieties. The first lot are tax avoiders and the second lot are tax evaders. People in both groups take the risk that the tax returns they submit will be found to be wrong. In the process, by seeking to retain for themselves money that properly belongs to the state, they are (since tax avoiders are exploiting unintended loopholes in the system) depriving the rest of us of those funds and are seeking to defeat the social objectives they could help achieve. That is why I generically term them tax abusers.

Tax avoidance, which lawyers, accountants and bankers (who are the people who tend to sell this abuse) habitually say is within the law, is essentially submitting a tax return when you're not sure whether what you have claimed is entirely legal or not, but with the chances being that if you are found to have got it wrong you will not have broken any law, even if you have to pay some additional tax and a penalty as a consequence, to which no criminal sanction will apply. I stress that such behaviour is quite different from taking advantage of tax reliefs the law specifically permits. So, for example, if you pay money into a pension fund on which tax relief is due in accordance with the law, you are reducing your tax bill, but you haven't *avoided* any tax because the law says none was ever due. Tax avoidance and tax planning within the law should not be confused: they are not remotely similar to each other.

Tax evasion, in contrast, is submitting a tax return that you know to be untrue, either because it excludes income that should have been declared, or because expenses are claimed which are not appropriate for tax purposes. In both these cases criminal sanctions could apply to the person submitting the return, although that does depend upon them being caught. However, in most tax systems (the UK's included) people know that the odds of being caught evading tax are low, as they also are of being caught avoiding tax. What is more, those who do get caught may very well not be prosecuted. Tax avoiders and tax evaders both rely on the low odds of being found out and so both are abusive of the tax system.

So how do these abuses work and how do those perpetrating them get away with it? The first thing to say is that in very many cases these abuses can only be done by people whose income is not automatically declared on their behalf to their tax authority. This means that most employees are unlikely to be heavily involved in either tax evasion or tax avoidance whilst most businesses or self-employed people have the opportunity to be involved in one, the other, or both. It's also true that those who have investment and other sources of untaxed income also have more opportunity to partake in this activity. How they do it varies, depending on the sums involved.

Tax evasion is rife among the lowest-earning self-employed. They often hide their income by taking cash. Alternatively they may choose not to declare that they have any self-employed income at all to the appropriate tax authorities. There are more than 5 million self-employed people in the UK and even HM Revenue & Customs think at least 40 per cent of them under-declare their income, which is a figure that fails to take into account the number not declaring they are self-employed at all. Under-declaration of tax in this sector is, therefore, commonplace.[29]

Those with rather more income who are seeking to evade tax might form a company based in the UK to run a trade and then simply fail to file the accounts and tax returns that are due. I estimate that maybe 400,000 companies a year are doing this.[30] The resulting loss of tax runs to well over £10 billion, in my estimate. There are at present almost no mechanisms in place in the UK to detect this fraud.

Others evade tax by not declaring investment income, rental income (especially common in the buy-to-let sector), capital gains tax that is due, or inheritance tax that they may owe.[31]

And some use tax havens and offshore arrangements to hide their crime of tax evasion. In 2014, at long last, the government recognized the inherent criminality of this offshore abuse.[32] That, however, came too late to do anything about the considerable sums already stashed offshore by those who have been involved in this activity. In 2014 I estimated that offshore tax abuse cost the UK £4.8 billion a year. But, a word of caution is needed. Whilst it is commonplace to think that tax havens are the root of all evil when it comes to tax evasion this is not true. Total tax evasion in that year may, in my estimate, have come to £84 billion, so offshore is only a small part of the problem.

A common factor in all these abuses is the suppressing of information from view. What's surprising to most people is that this applies to a great deal of tax avoidance as well. Tax avoidance is hidden from view in a number of ways, but one of the most common remains the use of offshore structures including companies and trusts. In this case, however, the existence of the structure may well be declared to a tax authority, and it may even be the case that the nature of the transaction is disclosed; the gamble is that the tax authority will not have the time or resources to challenge the structure that has been created.

So why, in that case, is offshore used? As tax avoidance schemes often cost a great deal of money to put in place, it tends to be wealthy people and large companies who use them, and the sums involved in each tax avoidance transaction are bigger. High-profile people and large companies do not now wish to be publicly associated with tax avoidance because of the adverse publicity that tax campaigners (me included) have created about this issue over the last few years. (There is some academic evidence that suggests that some companies caught out not disclosing their offshore activities have subsequently increased their tax payments as if in reaction to that publicity.[33]) Offshore trusts and companies offer their users anonymity, since their names do not have to go on public record; similarly many public companies that use offshore rely on the fact that accounts of their offshore subsidiary companies do not have to be made available, to hide the extent of that activity from the public's eyes. In this way they explicitly hide the tax avoider from view, which is a key part of their attraction.

It is, however, important to note that, despite current public perception to the contrary, the total loss of tax resulting from tax avoidance is substantially less than the losses that arise from tax evasion. To put things in proportion, I estimated in 2014 that the loss to tax evasion in the UK might be more than four times greater than the loss to tax avoidance. HM Revenue & Customs think the ratio between evasion and avoidance might be only about 3 to 1, but in my opinion they dramatically underestimate the level of tax evasion. Whichever figure is closer to the truth it is obvious that evasion is the bigger problem.

Why do I include tax abusers among those who are seeking to deny the rest of us the choices that are available with regard to tax? In my opinion the minority of people in this country who evade or avoid tax are grabbing opportunity for themselves at cost to the rest of us. This is 'free-riding' the tax system. They do not want to give the state the money that really belongs to it, and are willing to take risks to keep that cash for themselves, and in so doing they are also seeking to deny everyone else the opportunities that are rightfully theirs. This is not a victimless crime. The honest majority are the victims of their abuse and that is true whether they avoid or evade. This action is usually completely deliberate. So, for example, Bournemouth University tax lecturer Richard Teather has written for the Institute of Economic Affairs (Margaret Thatcher's favourite think tank) that:

> *While I am not seeking to condone dishonesty or criminal activity, from an economic perspective this is merely another example of*

> *tax competition: indeed, it is often necessary*
> *behaviour in order to take advantage of tax*
> *havens. Without the willingness of some to*
> *engage in this sort of activity, tax competition*
> *would be much less effective and therefore*
> *reduce the benefits that flow from it for the rest*
> *of us.*[34]

This is about as close as I suspect anyone could have got to endorsing the process of tax haven abuse as a means to undermine the democratically elected choice of governments.

There is also the self-interest of the many advisers who sell tax avoidance to consider. The UK tax market of the big four firms of accountants is likely to be worth at least £2 billion a year in 2014. Of course, not all of this relates to avoidance, but nor are these firms by any means the whole market: there are 10,000 other firms of chartered accountants alone in the UK, and tax services are also provided by other types of accountant and lawyers and bankers. All these professions have generally shown remarkable reticence when called upon to back increased transparency in the tax system and there can be little doubt that this is because the opacity that makes it easier for them to sell tax avoidance provides them with considerable commercial advantage. I am not suggesting, even for a moment, that these professions do, in any way, willingly help tax evaders, but the fact is that by defending opacity for the purposes of tax avoidance they also assist those who use that same opacity for the purposes of tax evasion.

The result is that these professions not only seek to prevent reform to the tax system which would enhance the choices and options available to many in this country if only the right amount of tax were handed over to our tax authority of what is its rightful property, but also unwittingly assist tax evaders, who are an even bigger part of this problem.

To summarize: in my view three things are necessary if tax is to be used to best potential for the benefit of society as a whole. The first is that politicians must be better educated about tax, as should be newspapers and other media organizations who comment on this subject. There is no excuse for the continuing misunderstanding of the role that tax has to play in our economy, and what the impact of non-payment is. In particular, arguments for austerity for austerity's sake must be recognized to be as hopelessly wrong as they really are.

Secondly, the threat to democracy itself from those who promote flat taxation and who seek to take away the choices that tax enables within our economy must be highlighted to everyone who believes that the political process has to be based upon the right of people to choose.

Lastly, tax systems have to be designed to make sure

that those who seek to abuse them – whether in ways that they would argue are within the law, or whether by overtly criminal practices – are prevented from undertaking such activities, which represent selfish greed on the part of those who wish to free-ride the system at a cost to everybody else to whom opportunities are denied as a result.

All three groups perpetrating these errors of judgement deny well-being to the majority in this country. It is up to all of us to make sure that these mistakes are put right.

5

Tax and choice

By now you will have realized that I think tax systems are so important because, along with government spending priorities, they are the best mechanism by which an elected government can embed the social values it represents in the economy that it is charged with managing.

What you will also have realized is that if any government wants growth and a balanced budget then it hasn't got the option of withdrawing from the economy for which it is responsible. It instead has to, firstly, engage in that economy and, secondly, has to decide precisely what that engagement is all about. It is an act of folly, verging either on irresponsibility or an abandonment of democratic duty, for any government to do otherwise.

What that then means is that some tough decisions have to be made about tax, taking into consideration the discussion in Chapter 2 on just what tax is, that in Chapter 3 on why governments tax when there are other options available to them, and the analysis in Chapter 4 on the nature of money and how fiscal policy (or the management of the government's deficit) inextricably links tax, money and economic management together, whether some would like to claim otherwise, or not.

The result is that making decisions on tax can either be seen as an enormous burden in addressing the near impossible problem of guessing right now what action is needed to deliver future well-being, the outcome of which decisions will inevitably be disappointing on occasion, or it's an enormous and liberating opportunity to build the future that people want and which politicians can, and should, offer. Unsurprisingly, I take the latter view and I guess it's my hope that I can persuade you to share that view, or I wouldn't have written this book.

At least three conclusions flow from these observations. The first is that tax and morality are inextricably linked: it is impossible for moral judgement to be removed from decision-making on tax.

Second, because decisions on tax are, hopefully, subject to democratic scrutiny then tax is always and inextricably political.

In turn this leads to the third, and obvious, conclusion, which is that no debate on tax can ever be objective.

Any consideration of tax issues is always, and inevitably, subjective whether those engaging in it accept that is the case or not. We all bring our own value judgements, life experiences, prejudices, hopes and principles to all aspects of tax. Those who say otherwise are deceiving themselves, are lying or are economists (and a Venn diagram might indicate some serious overlaps between those categories).

Might I suggest those three conclusions are just about the only incontrovertible statements in this book? I think they are right. Everything else, pretty much without exception, you can disagree with and it does not prove me wrong: it just proves we disagree. That in itself means that my claim that tax is all about choice has, by definition, to be right. And choice means we have to decide (which is what the rest of this book is about).

In that case we should want those decisions to be the best and most informed they can be. To achieve this, it is crucial that the process used for the decision-making is the fittest for the purpose. It is important, too, to identify what constraints there might be on what we can decide. I believe there are some fundamental pre-conditions for the existence of a good tax decision-making process in any society which, if they are not met, will result in a tax system that fails to meet people's expectations.

Education – the first condition for a good tax system

It is absolutely essential that people understand what tax is, what it can do, what options are available, how a tax charge is created, how it works, and in turn is accounted for, how it is enforced, and what recourse is open to anyone who thinks the tax system has treated them inappropriately or unjustly. For a topic that most will have never seen discussed in a tax book that is a long list of issues to consider, but some have already been addressed in this book. So I have, for example, already discussed what tax is and what it can do. I have also explained how tax impacts on the economy.

What I have not yet said is that I think it vital that these issues – including views that differ from my own – be widely understood and taught in schools, colleges and universities. I am amazed that is not already happening, when for a period of more than fifty years the UK government has collected one third or more of our national income in tax. In 2014, according to the HM Treasury budget, that total will exceed £600 billion for the first time. Tax, then, is at the heart of our economy. Indeed, tax is at the heart of our society. But we do not talk about it, and we do not teach it, and that is little short of a national scandal.

The result of this glaring omission is that it is all too easy for some to represent tax as simply a 'bad thing' that one can only ever want to make as low as possible, irrespective of the consequences. That shocks me and leads me to ask if that is the best we deserve. Surely something a little more serious is required on an issue so important we contribute a third or more of our national economy to it?

It is astonishing how little attention UK universities pay to tax. In June 2014 I searched the 'Which? University' website for undergraduate courses. When I asked for a course in accountancy I was offered 573 courses at 122 universities. When I asked for a course in tax the response was 'We're sorry but we couldn't find any results to match your search terms. Check the spelling or try a broader search'. If medicine is ultimately the study of death then death gets 406 courses at 89 universities but the other supposed certainty in life is apparently worthy of none. Now in noting this fact I am not saying that I believe that there should be a rash of new undergraduate courses in taxation. But I am saying I think the academic study of tax woefully inadequate in the UK at present and, given its central role in the under-standing of so many other subjects, that an understanding of tax should be an essential component of courses on, for example, medicine, social work, politics, economics, philosophy, sociology, education and much more besides. How can any of these subjects be properly understood if the environment in which they exist and are funded is not appreciated? For the same reason, I think tax should be a compulsory part of the school curriculum. Our collective ignorance about tax has to be banished, and along with it the negative attitude that prevails. Only education can do that, and it's fundamental if we're to have really informed decisions on tax.

Research – the second condition of a good tax system

Informed decisions are impossible without access to the relevant information: we must have good research into the options available to us when we come to make decisions on tax. The sad fact is that we are a very, very long way from achieving this goal right now.

HM Revenue & Customs does, of course, undertake some research on tax in the UK, but almost entirely within the constraints of the systems that we already have. They also have to work with incredibly limited budgets; so much so that almost no tax decision is reviewed after implementation to ensure that it achieved its stated objectives. We have, in effect, a state tax authority with no feedback loop within its own research systems to review success and failure. No wonder mistakes have been made time after time after time.

In addition to HMRC we have one major tax research centre in the UK, which is part of the Said Business School at Oxford University. Unfortunately this Oxford Centre for Business Taxation is heavily funded by big business[1] and, whilst it would be good to think that this has no influence upon its research output, in my opinion that is not the case. There is, unfortunately, no equivalent centre anywhere else in the UK (which in itself makes my point about a lack of research) and there is as a result significant crossover between this Oxford centre and the Institute for Fiscal Studies on policy issues (such as the Mirrlees Review on the future of tax design[2]). So strong is this relationship in fact that it is easy to see the two bodies as synonymous at a policy level. That was uncomfortably illustrated when one of the principal authors of the Mirrlees Review section dedicated to corporate taxation,[3] Professor Michael Devereux of the Oxford Centre for Business Taxation, argued in the *Financial Times* in December 2012 that 'The best reform of corporation tax would be its abolition'.[4] That hardly looks like a view wholly independent of the interests of some of his major funders.

Whilst it is, of course, the case that there are other tax researchers at other UK universities, and even a body called the Tax Research Network that apparently provides opportunity for them to highlight their work, these academics have been noticeable only by their absence from the very significant tax debate that has fired public imagination in recent years and it is rare indeed that any are called to give evidence to Parliament.

Talking of Parliament, it too is without adequate research resources on this subject. The House of

Commons Library does produce some useful papers, occasionally, but they are only literature reviews. More importantly, critical committees such as the Treasury and Public Accounts Committees do not have research budgets to ensure that the information they are given by bodies like HMRC is credible. This is absurd, and in marked contrast to the USA, for example. How can MPs pass good tax legislation when they have so few resources available to them to ensure appropriate questions are asked on tax (or any other issue, come to that)?

In 2009 when the UK's Department for International Development wanted to review the available research literature on tax evasion, tax avoidance and tax expenditures in developing countries it had to ask a professor at the Oxford Centre for Business Taxation to do the work and almost all the literature he found was prepared by NGO researchers[5] – of whom, I should add, I was one. There is nothing wrong with NGO research, but the fact that in some quite critical areas (including studies on the UK tax gap – the difference between the amount of tax that should be paid in the UK and the amount that is actually paid – where my own work is just about the only available alternative to that offered by HM Revenue & Customs[6]) there is no material from other sources is dismaying given the importance of the issues in question. More research is needed if all the options that are really available to us are to be understood and the decisions that politicians are being asked to take are to be properly appraised.

Proper policy preparation

Good tax law requires that a government offer soundly thought-out draft legislation to a parliament for approval, with well-reasoned arguments being given in its favour and with proper costings of likely impacts being stated. Given how important tax is you would think that this would be the least that could be expected of the Treasury, which is, after all, the most powerful department in government. Unfortunately, you would be wrong. The vast majority of documents issued by the Treasury in support of their policy proposals either reiterate proposed legislation in slightly plainer English without offering explanation, or seek comment on a prescribed set of questions that inherently support the intended proposal. Impact assessments rarely reveal the basis on which they are calculated, or the ranges of uncertainty within which they were prepared. Assessment of outcomes is almost unknown.

All of these issues compound some of the fundamental problems inherent in the way in which we create tax law in the UK. One of these problems goes back a very long time, and is the consequence of a decision made in the House of Lords as long ago as 1869, when a judge named Lord Cairns said:

*If the person sought to be taxed comes within
the letter of the law he must be taxed, however
great the hardship may appear to the judicial
mind to be. On the other hand, if the Crown,
seeking to recover the tax, cannot bring the
subject within the letter of the law, the subject
is free, however apparently within the spirit of
the law the case might otherwise appear to be.
In other words, if there be admissible in any
statute what is called an equitable construction,
certainly such a construction is not admissible
in a taxing statute.*[7]

We do not have a lot to thank Lord Cairns for: what he
in effect said was that every 'i' must be dotted and every
't' must be crossed or there is no hope of recovering tax
in the UK. The upshot is that every year hundreds of
pages of tax law are produced to plug unintended loopholes in earlier legislation, that some lawyer or
accountant, somewhere, has lit upon as a means to avoid
tax without infringing 'the letter of the law' – abusing
the intention of Parliament, as Lord Cairns permitted
them to do.

It is true that in 2013 a tax General Anti-Abuse Rule
was introduced in the UK[8] (in the creation of which I
played a part) which had the intention of overcoming
some of the problems that Lord Cairns created, but in
my opinion the time has come to change our whole

approach to tax legislation in the UK and put it onto what is properly called a purposive basis. Every tax law would have attached to it a statement of exactly what it is meant to achieve and there would be a requirement that whenever a tax official or a court has to interpret the law they do so in accordance with the stated intention of the legislation. We could then massively simplify our tax law, because we would not need to anticipate every single possibility that might arise and make provision for it when drafting legislation, but could instead depend upon reliable interpretation of the intention of Parliament to deal with any future dispute over ambiguities. Another immediate and obvious advantage would be that those members of Parliament who are not trained lawyers or tax specialists would have some chance of understanding the legislation they are asked to approve, as would the rest of us.

There are yet larger problems inherent in the current structure of HM Revenue & Customs, which despite having the task of implementing legislation is also given effective responsibility for writing most of it on behalf of the government. The core difficulties have to do with a shortage of specialist knowledge and experience, and an inbuilt bias towards particular interest groups.

If HMRC is to undertake this work of preparing legislation and policy it should do so in a balanced and objective way, and yet the very structure of the department makes that highly unlikely. Not only are many of the executive, full-time, working directors of HMRC not tax specialists (including the chief executive at the time of writing) but the five non-executives all come from big business and two of them at the time of writing are former senior tax partners in Big 4 firms of account-ants.[9] This bias in favour of big business is not by accident; it is by design. Past statements by HMRC have suggested that it, or ministers, believe that it is only those with large-business experience who have the skills to be represented on this Board despite the fact that HMRC is also responsible for the taxation of smaller businesses, 30 million or so individuals and a host of other organizations, all of whom are, as a result of the bias in Board appointments, effectively excluded from representation in HMRC decision-making processes. Why those who lead unions, NGOs, charities, pension funds, pensioner organizations, small businesses and others apparently lack such skills is not clear.

That problem is exacerbated by the apparent shortage of experienced staff at HMRC, especially when it comes to creating tax policy. I have witnessed this at first hand on a number of occasions, firstly when representing trade unions in discussion at the Treasury when they were invited to such debates before May 2010, and more recently when invited in a personal capacity to sit on the advisory panel helping write the General Anti-Abuse Rule introduced in 2013. What is continually surprising is how inexperienced many of the staff in charge of taxation policy seem, whether they come from HM Treasury or HMRC (although the latter are usually better, for the obvious reason of having tax experience), and how dependent these departments are, as a result, on staff on secondment to either of these departments from big firms of accountants or lawyers. In one absurd situation draft UK government policy was being routed for discussion through PricewaterhouseCoopers email servers because the person serving as secretary to a committee was on secondment from that firm. Margaret Hodge, the chair of the House of Commons Public Accounts Committee, has raised this issue with regard to staff secondment from KPMG.[10]

Those same firms, the professional bodies of which they are members, and their multinational company clients, tend also to dominate the consultation processes that are supposedly central to the creation of UK taxation policy, again suggesting that there is considerable bias in the way in which this tax policy is prepared. As Lord Joffe, a member of the House of Lords Economic Affairs sub-committee that scrutinizes Finance Bills, said in the House of Lords in July 2014:

On the basis of the evidence received, I agreed and supported all the sub-committee's recommendations. However, I was concerned about the very narrow base from which that evidence was drawn. There are some 420,000

partnerships of one form or another in the UK,
90% of which have three or fewer partners.
Despite that, the evidence that the sub-
committee heard was overwhelmingly from
associations, organizations and professional
advisers who represent large partnerships,
which probably make up less than 1% of all
partnerships. Professional advisers inevitably
had potential conflicts of interest in that some
of their members would benefit from a rejection
of the proposed changes in the law.[11]

There is very good reason to believe that the basis on which tax legislation is prepared in the UK is inappropriate and that it does, inevitably, produce legislation biased in favour of particular interest groups. In a democracy this is, surely, unacceptable and is a matter in need of urgent reform.

Proper scrutiny – the basis of good tax law

Deficiencies of expertise, resources and appropriate advice continue to hamper the decision-making when proposed tax legislation reaches Parliament, which is the only body that has the power to approve it. In the UK at present that almost invariably means the Westminster parliament, but the process of devolving tax powers to the Scottish parliament is well under way and such powers are also likely to be given in due course to the Welsh and Northern Ireland assemblies. There are demands for such powers to be given also to major cities, London in particular.[12] If and when this happens, the shortcomings in the system that are already evident at Westminster are likely to be exacerbated in devolved parliaments and assemblies – unless something is done to address them.

Because much of the legislation is written in language about as far removed from plain English as it is possible to get, I have on far too many occasions been called by members of Parliament who, tasked with looking at draft tax legislation, have had to admit that they have almost no idea what a particular piece of law has been proposed to deal with, and why, or what it might mean. I make no criticism of them for that: the shortcomings lie in the parliamentary briefings from HM Revenue & Customs, which in far too many cases are unhelpful (they frequently simply restate the proposed law, clause by clause, in slightly different language), and in many more are missing necessary information, such as the likely economic impact of what is proposed. In the face of this unhelpful approach from the government, parliamentarians need their own expert advice to work out precisely what they are being asked to approve, and yet, rare exceptions apart, the only resources they can draw upon are the same big firms of lawyers and accountants who have, all too often, been heavily engaged in lobbying for the particular form in which the legislation is already being presented.[13]

If we really want proper tax legislation then we must give parliamentary committees tasked with scrutinizing that legislation their own budgets so they can purchase their own independent advice from those who they choose to offer comment upon the legislation they're being asked to consider. Only then might we get good tax decisions.

The accountability of HM Revenue & Customs

Once tax legislation has been created you would think that the question of accountability for its enforcement would be an issue of little concern, but that is far from the case. In fact, HM Revenue & Customs is the only major government department for which no minister is responsible. It is true that the MP holding office as the Financial Secretary to the Treasury reports to Parliament on the actions of HMRC and there is no doubt that he or she can call in the department's permanent secretary for discussion if appropriate, but there is no official direct line of responsibility from that permanent secretary to that minister, or in turn to Parliament.

The reason for this is in the department's name: Her Majesty's Revenue & Customs is technically responsible to the Crown. As noted in Chapter 1, after centuries of dispute between kings, queens and Parliament it was resolved that no monarch could raise a tax without Parliament's consent, but to this day, in the obscure way in which the UK constitution appears to work, the revenue and duties collected remain the property of the Crown. The fact that the Crown is represented in this case by the First Secretary to the Treasury, who it turns out is the Prime Minister, does not matter: HMRC remains technically unaccountable to Parliament.

For a long time the MPs who have sat on the Treasury Committee of the House of Commons have appeared reluctant to claim power of scrutiny over HMRC's actions. It fell to Margaret Hodge MP and her Public Accounts Committee to take on this role in such spectacular fashion during the 2010–15 parliament. She has had to pioneer, despite considerable criticism (not least from colleagues on the Treasury Committee), a form of accountability for HMRC without having resources provided to her to do so, and all this in the face of Treasury indifference, and sometimes outright hostility.

It is, of course, time that this absurd situation ended. There should be a minister in charge of a department that has direct responsibility for HMRC and all its actions and that minister should be directly accountable to Parliament. Parliament should in turn provide its appointed scrutineers of that department with an adequate budget so that they can properly research its activities and hold it to account for both its successes and failures. Proper, functioning democracy should surely suggest that this change is essential.

Access to HMRC

The whole process of democratic government, if it is to function effectively, is dependent upon a set of checks and balances. Different countries create these in different ways. In the UK we create such checks by having two chambers to our parliament and by having a government that is drawn from the ranks of the largest party (or coalition parties) in the House of Commons, to which it is supposedly accountable through proper processes of scrutiny. Another essential element is the existence of a functioning legal system that can ensure that the law is enforced as intended, to which people can make appeal if they feel that injustice has been done.

By and large the UK has a reasonable track record here: people have the option of challenging HMRC's decisions in special tax tribunals and there is some assistance provided to help them do so. But there are problems before that stage is reached – which is the situation that impacts most people. If truth be told, for most people in the UK the real problem with tax decision-making is not how we ended up with the laws we have (which is the issue I have concentrated on up to this point in this chapter) but how they come to be asked for the amount of tax that is expected of them.

Once upon a time, which for these purposes I will call 30 years ago, HMRC ran a strong and vibrant system of local tax offices, with one located in just about every community of any size in the UK. There may have been historical reasons for this: systems were not automated and little communication was electronic, of course, so that having a letterbox through which people could put their correspondence to their tax inspector within the locality did, to quite a large degree, make sense. There was, however, something much more important than that in this local tax office network. What it recognized was that tax does, metaphorically, represent the price we pay for living in a democracy, and that if we are to see democracy in action in our communities we do, therefore, have to see our tax office present in the places where we live and work. That is what these local offices did. We were taxed by people we might have been to school with, and who were now our neighbours. We knew them, and, perhaps just as importantly, they knew us, and who the rogues were (including among the professionals with whom they had to deal). The system created local confidence, local effectiveness and local intelligence which was targeted at reducing the tax evasion that undermined the local economy. As a result, and of course on occasion a little grudgingly, the system worked quite well for all concerned, even if the rogues did not agree.

This was in the days when tax in the UK was run by

two independent departments, one called the Inland Revenue and the other HM Customs & Excise. The first department ran direct taxation, like income tax, corporation tax, capital gains tax and inheritance tax, whilst the second ran indirect taxes like VAT, customs duties, excise taxes and so on.

These two departments had very different attitudes towards their work. The Inland Revenue, by and large, presumed that they were dealing with tax-compliant people and maintained relationships that were respectful and which sought to resolve problems on the basis of understanding. Until its merger into HMRC, HM Customs & Excise (at least in my impression) presumed most people were crooks until proved otherwise, an attitude no doubt dating from their ancient origin as 'the Customs men' whose task it was to beat smuggling, on which many local economies were dependent in the eighteenth and even nineteenth centuries. (There were of course exceptions to the rule on both sides.)

Since the merger of the two departments there is no doubt that the old Customs attitude has prevailed within HMRC. Many who have to deal with HMRC think that the assumption that we are all crooks now prevails, quite widely. Worse than that, though, is the new department's change in attitude towards public service. As already noted, its Board has been deliberately dominated by people drawn from big business and its full-time directors have been recruited from outside tax departments, and the consequence is that HMRC has been seen, rather bizarrely, as a revenue-spending department within government even though it is, of course, and very obviously, the only really significant revenue-raising department government has. Despite the fact that over the last few years it has, to the annoyance of most taxpayers, persisted in calling those with whom it deals its 'customers', when that is the last thing that they feel they are, it has at the same time refused to entertain the idea that those 'customers' might ever be right or be deserving of something akin to a service.

The result has been all too obvious. With cost-saving made the department's absolute priority it has, between 2005 and 2015, cut more than 35,000 staff from its payroll, reducing the total number of employees from over 90,000 to about 55,000. There are now plans in place for further substantial staff reductions, with most of the job losses falling on those who actually deal with taxpayers, whether in person or on the phone.

Local tax offices have been closed in their scores across the country, with a significant decrease in local knowledge as a consequence, leading directly (in my opinion) to a rise in tax evasion.

Just as worryingly, in 2014 all the HMRC local enquiry offices, where a person could go to meet revenue officials face to face, were shut, with up to 2,000 jobs prejudiced as a result, making a mockery of the claim that HMRC would provide an alternative service in people's homes instead. Telephone-centre staff with limited training have replaced local-based staff with expertise in the tax system, and now even these telephone staff are to be replaced with online computer-based enquiry systems. Taxpayers will be expected to navigate a set of frequently asked questions and pick out an answer to their query, whether or not it fits one of the pre-scripted scenarios.

The idea that in these circumstances any taxpayer can truly understand the decision-making of the tax authority that demands payment from them is very hard to sustain and alienation from the system is the inevitable consequence – which brings me right back to the point where I started this consideration of the necessary preconditions for an effective tax decision-making process. That starting point was the suggestion that there is an absence of education on tax within the population at large, and now, quite shockingly, within HMRC itself, where trained staff are being replaced by computers.

Transparency

Given the appropriate political will it is not difficult to achieve change. Creating that will is the challenge. Over the past ten or so years a group of us have campaigned to get rid of the secrecy that used to surround so much to do with tax – a secrecy aided, abetted and encouraged by tax havens and big business – and we have, by and large, won the greater transparency we have demanded, albeit imperfectly as yet.

Before I go into more detail, I need to take you through the process of tax, which, I have long argued, involves six stages:

1. You have to define the tax base, which is done by creating the law, broadly speaking, using the process that I've outlined above.
2. You have to find where the tax base actually is. So, for example, if you decide to tax wealth, but it's all hidden outside the country, then you'll have a particular problem imposing that tax.
3. You have to actually quantify the tax base: you have to be capable of putting a monetary value on what you are going to tax or it is very hard to tax it. This is more difficult than you might think, since a lot of accountancy is just too subjective to form a basis for taxation. For example, do you really know the value of the house or flat you live in, let alone the land it sits on? Until the arrival of web sites like Zoopla most people could only have made a vague guess at this, and then only if there were other nearby houses of similar type they could compare. Even now such estimates may be wildly inaccurate in some cases.
4. You have to ensure that the right rate of tax is

applied to the right tax base at the right time to
collect the tax owing. This requires a strong tax
administration.

5. Government spending that creates the need for tax
in the first place should be properly allocated in
accordance with a budget (something we are good
at in the UK).

6. All of this process should be accounted for openly,
and with due reporting back to the parliament that
approved the tax in the first place, or the
democratic principle fails (something we're really
bad at).

The issue of finding where tax bases are hidden has
been the subject of a virtual revolution over the last
decade. If, for example, in 2005, near the start of our
campaign, anyone had called for a wealth tax many
people would have laughed at the idea, because, as was
widely known at that time, it was really easy back then
for almost anyone to take their assets out of the UK and
locate them in a tax haven, after which there was almost
no prospect of that wealth being traced. What is extraordinary is that over the last few years this has changed,
or is in the process of changing, for a number of
reasons.

Although I was told as recently as 2009 by the UK
Treasury that there was no chance of what is called
automatic information exchange of data on the accounts

held in tax havens by UK residents taking place in my lifetime, it is now going to happen, with all the benefits of it flowing through to the UK's HMRC in the next few years at the latest. What this means is that if a UK resident has any interest in a bank account, company, trust or other arrangement in one of a whole list of tax havens, including all those operated under UK control such as Jersey, Guernsey, the Isle of Man, the Cayman Islands, the British Virgin Islands, Bermuda and more, then that place will have an automatic and legal responsibility to report the fact through their governments to HM Revenue & Customs. So suddenly what was hidden in these havens completely beyond view will become transparent. And the same transparency is also being created across the EU and beyond. The change is dramatic, and very welcome.

But the change is not restricted to the tax haven world. Again, pretty much as a result of the work of tax campaigners like the Tax Justice Network and Global Witness, pressure has been brought to bear on the UK government and the governments of many other places, including tax havens, to ensure that their registries of companies include details of the beneficial owners of those companies and not just those persons who lend their name as nominees to be recorded on public record. This is another vital development because it will make it much harder in future to disguise the ownership of a company in any country, including tax havens; and consequently money flows designed to avoid or evade tax can be more easily traced.

These measures on beneficial ownership of companies are not yet comprehensive enough: it seems unlikely that this information will be placed on public record, where it would be available to people who trade with these companies, and who need to know it. However, it is another step in the right direction and signals that further progress in due course is possible.

Finally, on the transparency agenda, in September 2014 the form of accounting for multinational companies called country-by-country reporting[14] received the endorsement of the Organisation for Economic Co-operation and Development for use for tax reporting purposes.[15] As a result it is likely that over the next few years all countries with the headquarters of a multinational corporation located in their territory should be supplied with a full set of the corporation's accounts broken down on a country-by-country reporting basis. That country receiving the data will then be expected to share that information with a wide range of other (but not all) countries in which that group trades; the exceptions being countries which do not have tax information-sharing agreements with the country in which the head office is located.

The country-by-country reporting data will include sales (split between those to real customers and those to other group companies), the number of employees, profit, tax provided for in the accounts as well as tax paid, and the net investment in the jurisdiction by the group. The object of the exercise is simple: to show if there is a mismatch between the apparent scale of the operation of the multinational corporation in a country and the profit it declares there. This is done by estimating the scale of real economic activity in the jurisdiction based on sales, number of people and assets, and comparing that data with the profit allocation to it. The method is not perfect of course, and is not a basis for taxing in itself. What it does do is provide an indication of whether a tax authority needs to investigate a company in more depth and if so in which jurisdictions investigation needs to take place. This might happen, for example, if the country-by-country reporting accounts of a multinational corporation showed a significant part of its profits arising in, say, Luxembourg or Jersey, even though it appeared that the level of sales in that place was very limited, as was the number of staff. In combination these factors might suggest that profit-shifting into the low-tax jurisdiction was taking place which required investigation to ensure that tax liabilities were properly stated in countries where the trading was really happening.

Although it is very firmly intended by the OECD, which has oversight of international tax rules, that this data not be made available on public record at present, the EU has not accepted this line and has demanded a limited form of this data be published by EU banks from July 2014 onwards. In my study of this data, which was published in July 2015,[16] I showed that there was very clear suggestion of profit-shifting taking place, with billions of euros of profits appearing to be reallocated by just seventeen EU banks to places like Belgium, Luxembourg, Singapore, Ireland, Jersey and the Isle of Man, all of which have reputations as tax havens, and away from countries like Germany, the Netherlands, the UK and Spain.

Unsurprisingly, the reaction from big business, and most especially that based in the USA, has been furious.[17] Those who have gained enormously from using tax havens and from the secrecy that corporate accounting, combined with tax haven opacity, has been able to create do not want to give up the benefits without a fight, but the moves are all against them. It is widely thought that country-by-country reporting will be voluntarily disclosed by many companies within a few years, paving the way to mandatory publication by all multinational corporations. The days of dark dealing may be coming to an end.

So what has all this to do with the question of choice regarding taxation, which is the theme of this chapter? The answer is that these reforms have made available many choices that even a decade ago were unimaginable. It is true that more progress can be made in many of these areas. For example, it is absurd that information is now to be supplied to HMRC on the use that UK-resident people make of companies located in tax havens when the same information is not at present supplied by UK-based banks to HMRC. Still, the precedent set internationally makes it easier to secure national legislation that will provide our tax authorities with the information they need to track down the owners of companies that might owe tax. And these data transform the way in which we can tax and so the options available to us. We can now decide what and how we want to tax, and put the procedures in place to do so, with much greater confidence than has ever existed before that we can actually charge the resulting taxes with a good prospect of them being paid. This creates a new era in taxation. And that in turn creates another exciting possibility, that tax can become the fault line in the political system where real political choice can be made, including at the ballot box.

6

The underpinnings of a good tax system

In Chapter 5 I argued that tax was about choice, and that, if we wanted it, that choice was now available to us. Choice is, however, something with which most of us feel uncomfortable. Choice is pretty easy to handle if the question is whether or not we want to go to see a particular film tonight. In that case the options available are clearly defined and the consequences rarely extend beyond upsetting the person asking, if we choose what they think to be the wrong option. But when the question is about what sort of tax system we want the options are not so narrowly defined and the choices available for making decisions are really wide.

The 2014 referendum campaign on Scottish independence offered a small insight into the complexity of the decision-making processes we might go through when considering how to exercise choice on tax. Although the question on the Scottish ballot paper looked innocuous enough (it was just six words and asked, 'Should Scotland be an independent country?') the range of emotions and of issues discussed as people tried to make up their minds was enormous.

National currencies, tax systems, the economy, benefits, membership of the EU, defence, energy needs, the desirable level of state spending, and much more came up in debate. Despite that what was never quite clear from either side was what were the guiding principles that drove their desires (bar an obvious feeling among many voters that Scotland could be trusted to run its own affairs whilst others clearly thought it could do better by remaining in partnership with the other countries in the UK). What decision criteria should apply to such a choice? And how are they specified? That's the tough point where rationalization of gut instinct becomes hard.

Tax evokes questions that are as complex. Leaving aside the question of statehood for a moment (because I will return to it later) what really matters when it comes to tax is that everyone involved understands what the principles underpinning a tax system are. I am talking here about the principles of the system as a whole and not just those of its administration – an area of debate that has seemingly been neglected for a very long time.

Adam Smith did address this issue, way back in 1776,

in his book *The Wealth of Nations*[1] in which he suggested four maxims for tax. Extraordinarily these maxims are still widely cited, as if unanswerably correct, today, largely because no one seems to have tried to replace them. They are worth quoting (each extract below being based on the original text, but shortened to contain only its key elements):

1. *The subjects of every state ought to contribute towards the support of the government, as nearly as possible, in proportion to their respective abilities; that is, in proportion to the revenue which they respectively enjoy under the protection of the state.*

2. *The tax which each individual is bound to pay ought to be certain, and not arbitrary. The time of payment, the manner of payment, the quantity to be paid, ought all to be clear and plain to the contributor, and to every other person.*

3. *Every tax ought to be levied at the time, or in the manner, in which it is most likely to be convenient for the contributor to pay it.*

4. *Every tax ought to be so contrived as both to take out and to keep out of the pockets of the people as little as possible over and above what it brings into the public treasury of the state.*

To put it another way, these can each be summarized in a single word:

1. Equity
2. Certainty
3. Convenience
4. Efficiency

Several points arising from these maxims are worth noting. The fourth maxim, for example, supports the view that there is no sense in running a government budget surplus. The first makes it very clear that the tax relationship is by no means one-way traffic: for example, Smith realized the imperative of having a functioning state if wealth is to be created.

That said, of these maxims (as Smith himself called them) only the first deals with the goals of the system as such. The others largely relate to its operation, and so concern matters I discuss in more depth in Chapter 7. The only real principle Smith offered was equity. If one had to make a choice of a single principle to guide a tax system, equity, or equality as we might now call it, might be a very good one, but it is a somewhat limited basis for a whole tax system: there must be more principles underpinning a modern tax system than that if appropriate choices are to be made as to its design. I suggest it is time to move on from Adam Smith and that there are at least four such further principles we need to take into account, which are:

1. Peace
2. Equality
3. Truth
4. Simplicity[2]

You can call them PETS for short, but I am not sure I would. Each, I think, suggests an idea that is critical to the creation and success of a modern tax system.

Peace

Let me get the glaringly obvious out of the way first, and say I realize that throughout history war and tax have been intim-ately related. Indeed, at one time war was the major reason for tax and it should, therefore, be no surprise that, as noted in Chapter 1, Magna Carta limited the king's right to tax precisely because he had been demanding tax to fund wars that were unpopular with his barons.

If war and tax are linked in that way so, by obvious implication, are peace and tax. Peace reduces the amount of tax required to be extracted from an economy. The relationship is almost that simple, and most would think that this outcome would be a good thing.

That said, even the most fundamental of libertarian thinkers seems to think tax acceptable if it relates to the maintenance of law and order and the preservation of private property rights (some of them seem to think there is little further role for government); but if you look on these two goals as 'keeping the peace' then you have a further link between tax and peace.

However, in proposing 'peace' as a principle to underpin the tax system I am using the word to represent something much more than these rather limited aspirations. It is my belief that tax is a fundamental mechanism used to reconcile society's conflicting economic goals and needs, because the way in which tax is collected does, in my opinion, both reflect and shape the society that charges it. No society can survive for long without reconciling these goals unless it resorts to oppression.

This reconciliation is possible, in my view, because tax represents the 'consideration' paid by people who live in a country in exchange for the social contract that exists between them, its government, and each other. There is mutuality implicit in that coexistence, but necessary mutuality almost inevitably gives rise to conflicts, some of which will be economic. It is my belief that tax can and should reduce the risk of such conflicts by reducing inequality in society, using resources more equitably, making sure all basic needs are met and at the same time providing people with access to the means to make their own livings in the way that they want; and, if that outcome is achieved, then economic conflict is less likely and so peace will result.

The other three of my fundamental principles also have a role in achieving this reconciliation. Greater equality in a society clearly reduces tension. Simplicity, if it increases understanding and certainty, does the same, whilst truth is the bedrock of trust, which is the foundation for peace. My themes aren't unrelated. But there is more to the peace that tax can bring than that. Tax is about buying into the society of which we are a part.

That is why, as I explained in Chapter 2, paying tax is a voluntary act for most of us. And that is why not paying tax due is seen as an affront to those who have paid, which is why we have laws to punish those who deviate from the norms that society imposes. The overwhelming majority of us want to live in harmony, and accepting the role of government, and its right to tax, is part of accepting the mutuality that really does underpin successful communities.

The concept of mutuality can be extended to the international level. It is dangerous to suggest, as many do, that we should promote tax competition between states, since all competition is necessarily predicated on the idea that it is acceptable for participants to fail. We cannot afford failed states and anything that even hints at that possibility has no place in the international tax system. That does not mean that international uniformity is necessary, but cooperation and, where appropriate, harmonization are essential if tax is not to be an instrument for one state to exercise control over another. It is no coincidence that those who propose tax competition are the ones who are seeking to exercise that control. Time and again right-wing think tanks have made statements like the one below from Dan Mitchell of the US-based Center for Freedom and Prosperity, writing on this occasion for the UK-based Adam Smith Institute.

> *Tax competition exists when people can reduce tax burdens by shifting capital and/or labour from high-tax jurisdictions to low-tax jurisdictions. This migration **disciplines profligate governments** and rewards nations that lower tax rates and engage in pro-growth tax reform.*[3]

The emphasis is mine, and appropriate. Think tanks like those Mitchell works for go out of their way to defend tax havens.[4] And what they are really saying is that tax havens should be able to use their laws to undermine the tax laws of other states by inducing the relocation of economic activity to low-tax jurisdictions.

There can be no doubt that some low-tax states – like Ireland – have induced some real companies to relocate real economic activities through the offer of low taxes. But even places like Ireland are also part of the tax haven activity which induces no real change in economic activity at all, merely the relocation for tax purposes of where accountants record the profits of the companies for whom they work. This process is called profit-shifting.[5]

Profit-shifting is, I stress, a pen-pushing exercise, usually backed by a lot of paperwork. Perhaps the biggest single exposé of the activity to date came from the Luxleaks disclosures in late 2014.[6] The key issue there was secrecy, as it always is in these cases. Large companies secured tax advantages from the use of obscure Luxembourg subsidiaries that had little or no economic substance to them, where the detail of what they were doing was hidden from the states who lost tax as a result.

This is the reality of tax competition from tax havens that right-wing think tanks promote on behalf of their corporate funders. In most cases tax havens are better described as secrecy jurisdictions.[7] They are places that intentionally create regulation for the primary benefit and use of those not resident in their geographical domain, that regulation being deliberately designed to undermine the legislation or regulation of another juris-diction. To make sure that, as far as possible, those trying to avoid the regulation of their home country cannot be identified, the secrecy jurisdiction also creates a deliberate, legally backed, veil of secrecy that ensures that those from outside the secrecy jurisdiction making use of its regulation cannot be identified as doing so.

This, of course, is exactly what Luxembourg did in the Luxleaks cases. Most of the tax scandals of recent years have revolved around this tax haven secrecy being used to hide the artificial relocation of profits. Google moved profit to Bermuda behind a veil of secrecy; Starbucks did much the same to Switzerland via the Netherlands; and Amazon did it to Luxembourg: the theme is always the same.

This is not true competition or anything like it. Any economist knows that fair competition requires that all the participants have available to them all the information they need to make an informed decision. Tax competition works in exactly the opposite way, and hides from view everything that it can, which reveals what this activity really is: it is economic warfare waged from tax havens that are places that have sold their right to legislate in order to facilitate attacks on the law of other countries, and then provide secrecy to ensure that those involved cannot, as far as possible, be identified.

No wonder then that peace is such an important word for tax. This tax war has to end, and cooperation is now essential or the whole foundation of the state, and its right to tax, will be undermined and with it will go all the activities on which so many depend, because the right to choose them will be lost as democracy will also have been undermined.

All this suggests that the principle of peace, when it comes to taxation, has a lot to offer internationally, but there are other gains to be had at a domestic level. Most importantly, tax, and the spending to which it is linked, has to settle the futile war that has waged for far too long between left and right, and between pragmatists and dogmatists, on whether the state or the private sector is better at doing certain things, when the reality is that each has its very obvious strengths in some situations, just as it also has very obvious weaknesses in others. If peace means creating sufficient harmony for potentially conflicting parties to co-exist and tolerate each other then there are gains to be had in resolving these differences.

Take for example the idea few would question that a tax system should encourage innovation, skills and enterprise. That seems like a statement of the obvious in the twenty-first century. And almost without exception people will presume that in saying so I am referring to an activity that takes place in the private sector; and yet, as recent research by Professor Mariana Mazzucato[8] has shown, many major technological developments that most people think have been created in the private sector have in fact resulted from government-funded research, including most components of the internet and mobile phone technology. Clearly it makes sense for tax to fund innovation, skills and enterprise wherever they are to be found, and whoever owns the entity where they occur; the ownership issue does not matter as much as achieving the desired outcome. This is a fact that a tax system should recognize: the goal of peace in that same system is to make sure that the party best able to undertake an activity should be chosen on ability, and not dogmatically. Tax should not set parties against each other when there is an outcome to be achieved; in fact it should do just the opposite.

Tax has to support business to undertake these tasks in the private sector, but also has, for example, to support the NHS, and the state-funded arts, and educational establishments, and so many others if and when they seek to achieve the same goals. We have to see this continuum from state to private sector, and from tax to subsidy if we are not to set parties against each other and so deny people the chance to deliver to their best potential, whatever type of organization they work in. Getting this right is about creating a harmonious and balanced economy: I think that might be called one at peace with itself. We're far from there right now.

Equality

Just as peace is a word fairly easily linked to tax, so is equality. Adam Smith was keen on it, after all. That said, as with peace this is an issue where I think we need to go beyond the obvious.

The obvious thing to say when it comes to tax and equality is that anyone giving more than a moment's thought to this issue would deem it essential that people on similar levels of income and in similar circumstances should, within the same society, pay similar amounts in tax irrespective of the source of their income. This, in taxation terms, is called horizontal equity. The trouble is that, while it might be obvious that horizontal equity is important, we are very bad at delivering it.

Horizontal tax equity would be easy to achieve if there was one type of income and maybe only one way to receive it, but life, of course, is not as simple as that. There is earned income, which can come from employment or from self-employment, and investment income, which can come from low-risk bank savings, high-risk dividend income, rents and a host of other sources. The state too can provide income to individuals, some of it taxable (such as pensions), and some which is untaxed (certain benefit payments, for example). All these possibilities create complications in the achievement of any logical horizontal equity in the tax system. What is more, there are ways to receive income through a company rather than as an individual; long ago, limited liability companies were invented, and they have traditionally had lower tax rates than individual people, although the reasons for this have been long forgotten in most cases. That too creates a distortion when it comes to horizontal equity.

All these issues need to be addressed if tax is to deliver all the advantages of which it is capable. Unless that is done, then, for example, the absurd situation can arise

Figure 8: UK tax paid by income decile, 2010–11

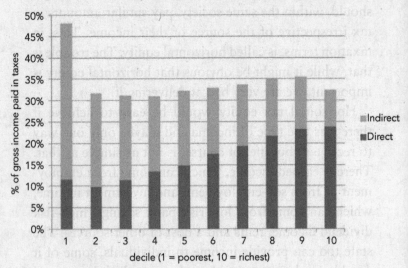

Source: Richard Murphy and Howard Reed, 'Financing the Social State: Towards a full employment economy', April 2013, Class Think Tank[9]

where a person who owns a company can receive within that company an income of £1 million in the year and pay tax of no more than 20 per cent on it, whereas another person generating the same income in the same way but who chooses to record it as individual earnings from self-employment could pay tax at more than double that rate in the UK at the present time. We are, as a result, a very long way from horizontal equity right now.

Horizontal equity is taxing income of equivalent amount at an equivalent tax rate; the other form of tax equality that is usually identified is vertical equity. Vertical equity ensures that a tax system is progressive, which means that the overall tax rate that a person pays increases steadily as their income rises. There are complications in achieving this goal too, in the first instance from the existence of state benefits, but also from the fact that the tax system as a whole is much bigger than the income tax system most people tend to think about. Figure 1 on page 32 gives a breakdown of the tax revenues in the UK in the year to March 2014 with the proportions each tax contributes to the total. Such is the complexity of all these varied taxes that it is now generally believed that in practice the tax burden in the United Kingdom is not progressive at all.

Figure 8 (see opposite page), based upon data from the Office for National Statistics for the tax year 2010–11, gives an indication of how the tax burden is distributed among income groups at present. In itself this chart shows the difficulty of delivering vertical equity in a tax system: when taxes on consumption are high (as they are in the UK when the combination of VAT, excise duty and other charges is taken into account) and those on low incomes spend all they have (and sometimes more besides because of untaxed income sources or borrowing), then what appears to be a partially regressive tax system results. In fact, the 10 per cent of people with the highest incomes in the UK appear to pay less in total taxation than many on lower incomes.

Equality may be the name of the game in tax, but we aren't delivering it – and that is taking into account only the obvious issues relating to tax and equality that most people tend to think of.

As I said at the start of this section, there is rather more to tax and equality than these obvious considerations. To presume that equality, when it comes to tax, is restricted to such technical issues as those already mentioned would be absurd. Tax has the means to shape society, including the degree of equality within it; and this is not just by the way a government taxes, but also by the choices made about what to tax (or not), what to give allowances to (and not) and what to spend state resources upon, or not. Taking this broader perspective, I would suggest there are three aspects of equality within society that should be considered in creating a tax system with equality as its guiding principle.

The first of these is that anyone must, if they are to have any chance of equality in life, have the basic means to participate in the society of which they are a part. If they cannot participate in that way there is clearly a total failure in terms of equality. This, I stress, is not an absolute measure: the material needs that must be met to participate in a modern society are somewhat greater than those required to simply stay alive. So, for example, in a society where everybody has a mobile phone, the person who cannot afford one is necessarily excluded. In 1990 it would have been impossible to say that a mobile phone was essential to participate in society; now it probably is. The material need that must be met to ensure equality is, then, a relative measure dependent upon time and place, and any tax system has to recognize that fact.

Beyond material need there is, secondly, the idea of equality based upon sufficiency. If a person is to fully participate in the society of which they are a member then they must have access to not just material well-being but also sufficient education, emotional support and both physical and mental well-being. It does of course depend on the individual whether they actually take up the opportunities, but unless the chance to access all of them is available, unconditionally, it is clearly impossible for it to be argued that equality exists.

Additionally, whilst any tax system should promote the opportunity for a person to earn their own, sufficient, living, there is equally an obligation inherent within that tax system to ensure that a person who cannot, for any reason, achieve that goal is adequately protected from the consequences and can still participate in society. In the first instance this means that the tax system must be flexible enough to reflect the way some people want, or have, to work. So, for example, it must embrace the twenty-first-century trend towards flexible employment, multiple jobs and a combination of self-employment and employment, in ways that have not happened to date. Secondly, it is clear that the tax and social security systems must be integrated to ensure that there is equality of treatment, which is not always achieved.

It is then important to note that this issue extends beyond mere cash payments to and from the individual. Ensuring availability of resources such as appropriate housing is an essential part of this process of achieving equality of sufficient well-being to participate in society, as too is a policy of full employment. It is pointless having a tax system that says it promotes equality of sufficiency but does not also promote the means to deliver it. One can, of course, extend this notion to education and healthcare as well as many aspects of the social welfare system on which so many depend at some point in their lives.

It follows that within this definition of equality is to be found most of the framework of what we call the welfare state. Indeed, if we extend the definition of sufficiency a little to cover not just a point in time but a person's well-being throughout their life then the entire welfare state system is included. And it is entirely right that equality of sufficiency to participate should not just relate to the current moment; it is a measure that has to exist, even as it changes, across time. So, for example, the young must be cared for by society, even though they cannot as yet contribute in a material sense towards well-being, and similarly the elderly must be provided for even if their current material needs were not antici-pated at the time that they were making active material contribution to the society of which they are a part.

In this context there is, I suggest, a fundamental inter-generational contract that says that one generation will look after the next in exchange for that next generation in due course caring for them when they are no longer able to contribute as once they did. This is the real basis for pension provision, however those in the financial services industry like to dress the issue up, and the tax system has to recognize that fact. What is more, equality of sufficiency for the elderly to participate requires that this obligation be met even when the outcome was not anticipated, as might be the case at present when increased life expectancy has significantly extended the average period of a person's retirement. Meeting these needs is not just contractual obligation: it is an equitable obligation as well, and any tax system has to reflect that.

It is also important to note that this concept of equitable obligation between generations extends beyond those generations already born. It is very difficult for most people to imagine making commitments well beyond our lifespans, and yet the latest grandchild of those in old age today might quite plausibly live for a century, and that grandchild's grandchildren if born during their old age might live for another century after that. In that case any expression of sufficiency must consider the needs of future generations for a long time to come, not least in setting limits on the impact the present generation can make upon this planet.

Survival and sufficiency are concepts relating to minimum expectations. With luck many people will have the opportunity to exceed their minimum expectations, will indeed have the opportunity to fulfil their potential and achieve personal goals. Individuals of course vary greatly in their talents, and their goals will be diverse. They will measure success or fulfilment by different criteria. This is where the concept of equivalence comes in – the third aspect of equality I want to discuss. Equivalence is about people achieving different things that have comparable worth in their own perception, and the diversity will include diversity of income. Equality of both sufficiency and opportunity demands that the contributions people make in tax differ according to the monetary surplus each has over the sum required to achieve sufficiency, so that equivalence can exist for the benefit of all in a society. Sufficiency is a base line in defining this contribution: equivalence is the goal.

Here, thankfully, there is theory that helps us, and it is equivalence and not equality on which we rely to come up with an answer on redistribution. What we know from economic theory, which can also be readily confirmed by life experience, is that as any person's income increases, the value to them of each additional pound, dollar, euro, yen or other currency that they earn reduces. The precise amount by which the value of each pound (etc.) falls could be the subject of endless and largely pointless debate, and it will vary from person to person and maybe from time to time, and the rate of change will not be consistent across a person's whole income range (by definition), but what is indisputable is that to the person who has an income of £10,000 an additional £1 is almost invariably worth more than that same £1 is to the person who has an income of £100,000. If that is true then it follows the loss of £1 to a person earning £10,000 costs them more in terms of the impact of the loss suffered than the loss of £1 costs a person earning £100,000. Since it is undeniable that paying tax does feel to some people like a loss of money, it follows that to achieve equivalence in the contributions made by people on different incomes, both the overall tax due and the marginal tax rate payable by the person with a lower income must be less than those charged on the income of the higher earner. Equivalence of contribution, measured by the loss suffered, demands that this is the case and as a result progressive taxation must be a fundamental feature of any tax system if it is to achieve the goal of promoting equality.

There is now a strong body of evidence that suggests that this approach to equality produces better outcomes for all the people in a society. We now know that more equal societies tend to be wealthier, healthier, happier and overall more prosperous than unequal societies. The work of professors Richard Wilkinson and Kate Pickett has been fundamental in establishing a common understanding of this seemingly obvious truth and although

Figure 9: The shadow economy in EU member states as percentage of GDP

	Size of shadow economy – %
Austria	7.5
Belgium	16.4
Bulgaria	31.2
Cyprus	25.2
Czech Republic	15.5
Denmark	13.0
Estonia	27.6
Finland	13.0
France	9.9
Germany	13.0
Greece	23.6
Hungary	22.1
Ireland	12.2
Italy	21.1
Latvia	25.5
Lithuania	28.0
Luxembourg	8.0
Malta	24.3
Netherlands	9.1
Poland	23.8
Portugal	19.0
Romania	28.4
Slovakia	15.0
Slovenia	23.1
Spain	18.6
Sweden	13.9
UK	9.7
Average	*18.4*

Source: Friedrich Schneider, 2013[10]

there are some economists who have challenged the way in which they have evidentially supported their claims the fact is that the vast majority of observers think these objections nitpicking, at best. The claims made by Wilkinson and Pickett in their book *The Spirit Level* represent truths that are self-evident to most of us.

But in that case the very real practical challenges in delivering equality, some of them already mentioned at the start of this section, have to be addressed if principles are to be turned into reality.

Truth

Truth should, if truth be told, be the foundation of all successful tax systems. All such systems are based on voluntary compliance, since there are never enough resources available to any tax authority to check the tax disclosures of all taxpayers. Unless there is honesty between the taxpayer and tax authority about what income and assets the taxpayer has that might need to be taxed and, in turn, honesty from the government about how the tax system works and for what benefit, then the relationships of trust that are essential in the tax system fail. The result of that failure is cost to all parties arising from burdensome regulation, as well as increased inequality as a consequence of people successfully cheating the system.

It would be fantastic if it could be said that this

dependence upon taxpayer honesty could be relied upon to produce correct tax returns, but that is not the case. The latest best estimates of the scale of the shadow economy – that part of economic activity not recorded, in order to ensure tax is not paid – in the EU member states are shown in Figure 9 (see p. 172).

It is ironic that some of the states on this list most associated with being tax havens (Luxembourg, Austria, Ireland, the Netherlands, and, yes, the UK) have some of the smallest shadow economies. Perhaps the irony is that they have less need to steal their own taxes since they're quite good at stealing other people's instead. Low as it may seem in percentage terms, however, the UK's shadow economy of 9.7 per cent implies unrecorded income of maybe £180 billion a year and tax lost of at least £70 billion as a direct result. Dishonesty is big business even in one of the relatively clean countries. When shadow economies reach the levels seen in some Balkan countries then the threat to the financial stability of the state as well as to the extent to which it can successfully intervene in its own economy is severely prejudiced, as has been seen in the case of Greece. No tax system is ever going to have the resources to pursue and enforce full payment of all the tax owed, so punishment of those deviating from the norm of making full payment will always in practice be the exception. From all this it is apparent that truth is an issue that has to be focused upon in any tax system if it is to be truly effective.

The aim of doing so can be simply stated: all tax authorities need to ensure the maximum possible voluntary compliance with the tax laws of the state to which they are responsible.

This might sound straightforward, but is significantly more multi-faceted than simply passing laws imposing draconian tax penalties. Indeed, if voluntary compliance is the aim, such laws almost contradict the objective of the system: the focus of attention has to be different.

The first such focus has to be on the political system. For a tax system to be successful the political system that promotes it has to be genuinely democratic, free of corruption and capable of delivering political leaders who can be considered trustworthy. The example has to be set at the top. If it is not then corruption filters downwards.

That then suggests the second issue of concern: a country's tax authority has to be staffed by people who are themselves considered to be trustworthy. If corruption exists, and becomes widespread within a tax authority, there is no chance whatsoever that the right amount of tax will be collected in that country. This issue is not unrelated to the first: it is only honest politicians who can command an honest tax authority for fear of it otherwise turning on them.

Third, every effort must be made to encourage tax-payer compliance with the rules of the system. This not only involves making sure that the obligations a taxpayer has to comply with are well known to them – which is a form of telling the truth in its own right – but also involves letting the taxpayer know that the tax authority can and does have means to check that they are being honest, and ensuring that such systems are actually in place. This last activity is far too little known about at present. It should, for example, be the case that a tax authority knows about all large bank deposits in people's bank accounts, and also about large purchases, such as houses and cars, so that these can be checked to see if they are consistent with declared incomes. And it should also be the case that tax authorities have access to bank data on the beneficial ownership of companies to make sure that when limited companies are used those making use of them can be properly identified and be held to account if they abuse tax law. Simple systems such as these, which make people aware that their chances of being caught cheating are high, will encourage truth-telling, even if a little persuasion is needed.

Domestic honesty is not, however, enough. The issue of tax havens, and the deliberate veil of secrecy that they provide to their users, has already been discussed in this book, and this has rightly been one of the main focuses of attention for those seeking tax justice over the last decade or so. There is not, and can never be (barring a threat to human rights, which would have to be tested on a case-by-case basis), a justification for refusing to supply information on income earned by the resident of one country in another place if that data is needed to ensure that tax is paid in the right place, at the right rate and at the right time, but that refusal is just what tax havens have long done, and might still seek to do despite recent efforts in this area by the Organisation for Economic Co-operation and Development, unless considerable effort is put in place to force their compliance. This then is one aspect of international honesty that needs to be tackled.

The other is the honesty of multinational corporations. No one really knows whether it was ever intended when limited liability was first made commonplace in the UK in the 1850s that one company should be capable of owning another, meaning that there could be layers of limited liability within a group of companies. What we do, however, know is that this has become the norm, with some conglomerates now comprising thousands of companies in many different countries. This creates a massive problem with truth-telling. The first problem is in even identifying what companies make up the group, which publishes one single set of accounts for its shareholders. So, for example, in June 2015 a report[11] found that Walmart has built an undisclosed network of 78 subsidiaries and branches in fifteen overseas tax havens. These subsidiaries had never been subject to public scrutiny before, in part because Walmart had not listed them in its annual 10-K filings with the U.S. Securities and Exchange Commission in the USA. The shareholders of Walmart might never have known that they had an interest in these entities but for that research. Similar research in the UK has also revealed many companies failing to list in their accounts or annual return filings to the UK regulator just which companies actually make up their group. This has meant that it has been almost impossible to find out the composition of some multinational corporations. This problem is compounded when subsidiaries have been registered in tax havens and have not therefore been required to place their accounts on public record, meaning that it is not possible, if a multinational corporation chooses this to be the case, to find out what activity is actually undertaken in many of the countries in which they might trade.

Awareness of this opacity within some of the world's most powerful corporations, including the complete absence of data on what tax they pay on a country-by-country basis, has given rise to a demand from 2003 onwards for the new form of accounting called country-by-country reporting, already referred to in Chapter 5.[12] The demand is that groups of companies tell the truth about who they are, where they are and what they really do. It would seem an obvious requirement but it has been fought tooth and nail by big business since the idea first began to hit headlines. Despite that in September 2014 the OECD made it the strongest recommendation to that date of its Base Erosion and Profits Shifting process[13] by saying that countries should demand this data to help them work out the risk in multinational corporations for tax purposes; the UK became the first to actually do so in 2015, and others have now followed. However, such was the business paranoia about the data, which may show just how sensitive the information really is, that companies persuaded the OECD that the data should only be available for private use by tax authorities, meaning most of the secrecy remains intact. Thankfully, tax justice activists from very many organizations, along with members of the European Parliament, have made clear that this is unacceptable, and as a result the European Commission remains under continuing pressure to force these data into the open, which I am sure will happen one day.

The message is a simple one: truth might underpin all taxation, but we are a long way from it being the norm. As a result the fight to secure it, as far as possible, so as to ensure that tax can deliver all the benefits it is capable of goes on.

Simplicity

Simplicity is the holy grail of tax design; it is what everyone seems to say they want and yet it's the thing that absolutely no one gets. There is good reason for that: the current complexity of our tax system is based on mutual mistrust. This goes back far into history.

Those who are taxed appear to have never trusted those who tax. It seems likely that the sentiment has always been reciprocated. The consequence is that complexity has been designed into the UK tax system from the outset, from which it has never recovered.

So, for example, when income tax was first created in something close to its current form in the UK in 1803 it was given what was called 'schedular form'.[14] There were five 'Schedules' labelled A (income from land and buildings), B (farming profits), C (public annuities), D (self-employment and other items not covered by A, B, C or E) and E (salaries, annuities and pensions). This has largely changed now (though only very recently), but what is important is to realize why the tax system was established in this way: the aim was to make sure that no one tax officer could know all the details of a taxed person's income. Opacity was a design feature of UK tax from the start.

As if this was not bad enough, UK tax law has, as has already been noted in some detail, developed on what might best be described as a 'strict legal' basis, when an 'equitable' basis would be of much greater use. This is a significant difference in a common-law country, which the whole of the UK is for tax purposes. A legal basis of interpretation of the law essentially requires that the words used in both law and in the way in which a transaction is constructed be looked at in isolation to determine whether tax law applies to them or not. In contrast (and I am aware I am simplifying matters a bit) an equitable interpretation of the law requires that the purpose of the law be established by a court, and the purpose of the transaction be reviewed, after which the way in which tax law is applied to that transaction is then interpreted in the light of both these things. It is indisputable that on occasions UK courts have swung towards this equitable approach to tax law, and have surprised everyone when they have done so, but the fact is that this is not the established way UK tax law works: the letter of tax law is what tax is based on and this has had enormous consequences.

The first such consequence is that because all language has imprecise meaning tax lawyers and accountants have sought to take advantage of the uncertainties in the wording of tax legislation to find loopholes that their clients can exploit. A vast amount of tax avoidance activity has arisen from this willingness of tax advisers and their clients to take a risk on the interpretation of law, which has been justified by their getting away with it on far too many occasions. Secondly, and as importantly, because no government has been willing to put a general anti-tax avoidance principle into UK law (although I did write one which was presented to the House of Commons by Michael Meacher MP as a Private Member's Bill in 2012[15]) all measures taken to beat tax avoidance activity have relied upon a process of laying tax law upon tax law to try to close loopholes, with the inadvertent consequence that on many occasions further loopholes have been opened, and the complexity of tax law becomes ever greater. That is why we now have tax law that grows by up to 1,000 pages of close type each year.

If we are seeking simplicity in taxation then the time for a principles-based approach to tax has very clearly arrived. Statements of principle by tax authorities on which taxpayers can rely are of particular importance in this regard: the mistrust on both sides, to some degree justified, has persisted for too long. The way to overcome this is to have purposive legislation: that is legislation that not only spells out the detail of how the law will work but also says what it is meant to achieve. The reason for that is to give guidance to taxpayers, their advisers and any court considering a dispute on how they can expect any law to be used. So if, for instance, a piece of law said it was intended to regulate the transfer of the ownership of property between spouses or civil partners, it would be obvious that this law could not be used to govern transfers between unrelated people, and any attempt to do so would be bound to fail. I have picked a simple example, but such clarity would stop many disputes, and would also, importantly, make it clear when HM Revenue & Customs is using law in a way that was not intended by Parliament, which has happened. Saying what a law is meant to do as well as how it is meant to do it is an obvious way of simplifying everyone's understanding of the law.

That said, simplicity in tax law will never be achieved and it may not always even be desirable. In a complex world rules will be required for complex situations and it is, I hope, by now very obvious from all that I have written that if tax is to achieve all the tasks that are expected of it then it will have to have a very broad scope – if only to give taxpayers the choices they need on such simple issues as whether to buy or lease a business asset.

At which juncture it is also important to repeat what was said in an earlier chapter, which is that what many people call a simple tax system – a flat tax system – might be anything but simple. Almost nothing is as it seems in taxation.

7
The policy decisions tax must impact

Tax does not exist in a vacuum. Nor is tax just about raising money. Tax should instead be a way that a government implements key elements of its vision for the society it wants to create on behalf of the people it represents. As a consequence tax policy cannot be decided upon in isolation, let alone be siloed in a Treasury; it must be integrated across the whole range of issues that the government wishes to address.

It is simplistic to say that there are four positions that might be taken on the role of government in the economy, but brevity requires that I reduce the options to be considered.

The first such position is that of the anarchist, who would argue that no government has the right to take a position of authority on any issue and as such should not engage in the economy. It's a position, but not one that I will consider further: I not only disagree with it, I also think it entirely impractical. So, I think, do the vast majority of people.

The second, third and fourth positions lie on one continuous spectrum. They move from the right-wing position that the state has to exist but should play as small a role in the economy as is consistent with the maintenance of law and order, defence and protection of the weak and vulnerable, through the position that has largely persisted in the UK for the last seventy years where the state thinks it has both the right and the duty to intervene to achieve a wide range of social and economic goals, to the socialist viewpoint, now little heard, that the state should not just intervene in the economy but own, control and manage large parts of it.

Just as I dismissed the anarchist position on the role of government so too am I going to dismiss the overtly socialist one that implies state ownership of much of the means of production, because I think it lacks the balance needed to make any society work. I also believe it has little mass appeal. That leaves two options on the political agenda when it comes to deciding upon the role of government, and so taxation.

If the volume and quantity of media comment was to be the basis for decision-making, rather than democracy, then the second option, of minimal state intervention, would appear at present to have much support. However, and at the same time, the media clamours whenever the state fails to fulfil a function that is seemingly inconsistent with this objective of minimal intervention. If one looks at what has actually been happening in government decision-making, observation suggests that the third scenario of a decidedly mixed state very largely prevails in practice, though with varying success as to outcomes.

The reality of UK politics (and that of much of the western world) is now about debate between parties who in practice compete for what they (by and large) describe as the middle ground, with dispute centring on just where the middle might be – but all set against an undercurrent of comment based on the minimal-state ideology of the right, which has rarely prevailed in practice, but which at present provides the only apparent alternative to a range of centre-ground thinking. The paradoxical duality in the stance adopted by the media reflects this situation.

All of this should be considered pragmatically. Whatever the claims made by those competing in the centre ground of politics and their more right-wing opponents, the reality is that collective experience has created an expectation of what the state might supply in the UK, against which the performance of any politician is measured. There is, for example, an expectation that there will be something approaching full employment, and that there will be economic growth that benefits most people, although there is indifference as to whether that growth comes from the public or private sector.

To support that growth it is assumed that the state will supply an education for all, now to the age of eighteen. Beyond that age the consensus has broken down, but on the other hand there has been broad agreement that state education might now start at three and not five: the loss in one direction has been largely compensated for in the other.

The role of the NHS is rarely questioned in the UK: the right to healthcare that is almost universally free at the point of supply remains almost beyond challenge, even if how it is supplied is a matter of some contention.

We also expect to be able to get to the NHS, education and work without interference: we expect the state to provide roads and, even if railways and buses are run by (state-subsidized) private enterprises, we expect the state to ensure that such services are available. It may be that we pay for elements of our transportation but it's government that we blame if the infrastructure to facilitate it is not present.

In just the same way, we blame the government for housing crises even when we do not now expect most homes to be provided by the state sector.

There is also a universal expectation that the state will supply law and order and national defence.

Regarding defence, expectations may have somewhat diminished, but on law and order they are growing. The scale of the threats from which we demand protection has increased enormously, from terrorism to cyber crime to paedophilia, and many of those, in turn, demand interventions across a much wider range of activity.

Changes in our ways of living have also produced new demands. We expect many more products to be safe than past generations could have conceived of, and get very angry if the government gets any such risk assessments wrong. Media comment may suggest that we hate 'health and safety', but the reality is that we are utterly dependent upon regulation to ensure we can safely consume products whose suitability we have no way of appraising ourselves.

We expect the state to remove and dispose of the rubbish we create, which moreover we now demand happens in an environmentally friendly way.

In all this we now also expect to make choices: the possibility is recognized that the option Scotland chooses may not be the one that England, Wales or Northern Ireland wants (and they may each be different too).

It's therefore no surprise that the demand for government services is remarkably consistent, and even if the government elected in 2015 thinks it can reduce the amount of GDP dedicated to the sector from 41 per cent to 36 per cent there are many (from the Institute for

Fiscal Studies onwards) who just can't make their figures stack.

As explained in Chapter 3, tax is not just about collecting money, but is itself, if the tax system is optimally designed, aligned to the range of social objectives I have just noted, with the deliberate intent of helping achieve these goals. So, in addition to raising revenue (or, more correctly, reclaiming cash already spent), tax must also:

1. Reprice goods and services to correct for market failures
2. Redistribute income and wealth
3. Reorganize the economy, and do so in ways that:
4. Raise representation in the democratic process, and
5. Ratify the value of money

And, as Chapter 6 made clear, all this has to be done within a framework that emphasizes:

1. Peace
2. Equality
3. Truth, and
4. Simplicity

That policy framework challenges much of the existing language of tax. So, for example, within this context efficient taxes are not just those that are cheap to collect per pound raised. And nor are they even the ones that necessarily raise lots of money, although there is no reason why either should not be true. Efficient taxes are those that best integrate tax recovery with government policy across the whole spectrum of its objectives.

As a result it cannot be said that there is such a thing as an ideal rate or combination of rates when it comes to any one tax if each of them is considered in isolation. That's because the amount that some taxes (such as income tax, VAT, national insurance and corporation tax) raise has such significant impact on the level of activity in the economy that this fact, and their interaction with other taxes, has always to be borne in mind when considering such issues. Design of these taxes is accordingly multi-faceted. You just can't debate the design of these taxes or the rates at which they are applied without thinking about both the micro and macro impacts simultaneously. Policy demands that you do.

So, for example, you wouldn't cut VAT and raise national insurance if you wanted to take the heat out of a consumption boom whilst wanting to give a boost to exports. The exact opposite behaviour would be appropriate if that was your policy goal because an increase in VAT usually cuts consumer demand, whilst cutting national insurance charges, especially for employers, can give exporters a potential cost advantage. And you might need to take this action to achieve the overall policy goal regardless of whether you felt the adjustment to either tax was desirable in its own right. This is precisely why flat taxes cannot work for a modern government: they are just not nuanced enough to meet its macroeconomic management needs.

Let me, then, draw some very clear policy inferences.

Inference no. 1

The total tax-take of the tax system as a whole has to be designed (as far as is possible) to suit the needs of the economy at a point in time. This is not about balancing the books. It is about giving the economy the amount of stimulus (or not) that it needs to ensure that there is maximum employment, growth and stability.

Inference no. 2

The way in which the tax-take happens is not neutral. The broad balance between taxes matters, so there must be enough of them. Having levers to pull is vital.

Having established those points let me stress that who pulls the levers also matters. It is now increasingly apparent that electorates think regionally and even locally as well as nationally. This is being matched by a demand for the increased devolution of taxing powers that must be met if the demand for representation is to be achieved. However, as the discussion of tax competition in Chapter 6 made clear, without care and without appropriately designed delegated authority there is a real risk that those granted the power to tax might be persuaded to use it to promote a form of competition that is, at the very least, unhealthy and even counterproductive. A race to the bottom in tax that can (and may be intended to) deny government the right to withdraw revenues from the economy, can mean that the scale of services supplied must be cut. There is enormous potential for conflict here that has to be avoided.

There are obvious ways to overcome this risk by good design that correctly matches policy and tax objectives. The first is to devolve the power to tax land to regional and local government. This has, of course, been long established in the UK as a whole, and for good reason.

The second way to prevent tax conflict is to avoid devolving the right to tax mobile resources. That means the right to tax most forms of capital wealth (excluding land) and most investment income has to be kept at national level because both these asset types can be so easily relocated. This mobility already gives rise to substantial problems with cross-border taxation and these problems would only be exacerbated if these tax bases were managed entirely regionally.

The third way to prevent tax competition within a state is to avoid devolving the taxation of companies because these can, notoriously easily, relocate their activities, as so many multinational companies have proved. Because countries around the world are already having to take so many steps to counter the negative impacts of tax competition for the corporate tax base it would be absurd to increase the risk of loss from this issue by devolving corporate tax responsibilities within the UK.

Fourth, there is good reason for not allowing the devolution of powers over sales taxes. This is because, once again, sales are so easily relocated, especially when made over the internet or when they are of services rather than goods. Sales taxes (including duties, which are especially susceptible to smuggling, as is common-place, for example, across the border between the north and south of Ireland) should be harmonized as much as possible and so not devolved.

Which then leaves the question, what's left to devolve? Apart from land tax, already mentioned, I suggest the presently suitable candidate is tax on income earned from work, which exists in two forms in the UK: income tax and national insurance. The sums involved when it comes to revenue from work are not that dissimilar in the case of these two taxes. There are several options for exactly how to devolve powers over these taxes, assuming both remain in use (and I note reasons for replacing national insurance later in this book). One would be to provide local control over the income tax base of the resident population by devolving the power to allow offsets against income. So, for example, regions might be granted the right to restrict some allowances to basic rates of tax – such as the allowance on pension contributions – or to deny them altogether. Another possibility would be to give regions limited rights to create new tax-free income streams if they relate to activities within their region, e.g. investment in collective housing schemes or local bonds used to fund regional infrastructure.

That said, whilst it continues in use it seems more logical to devolve one or both of employer's and employee's national insurance to localities in their entirety. It is relatively easy to locate most employees, and so 'cross-border' disputes could be minimized. In addition, there are few allowances and reliefs (excluding the exemption for those of retirement age) in national insurance so that what effectively is being devolved is a decision on rates. Companies operating in a number of regions would find it relatively straightforward to run parallel systems to cope with differing rates of national insurance, which would not be the case for income tax rates. A further argument in favour is that national insurance, being a tax on labour, provides an obvious counter to the taxation of capital tied up in land – which I am advocating should also be devolved locally – thus producing the balance of real political and economic choice to be exercised in local government that is vital to its credibility and the choice it has to offer an electorate.

There are other options that could also be added into the mix. So, whilst I definitely do not recommend that income or wealth taxes be devolved as a whole I do think that some of the many choices available within them could be made at a local level. For example, the option of charging additional taxes on rental income could be available as part of local taxation, and it may also be appropriate for all taxes on local rents to be accounted for locally. Control of allowances and reliefs against rental income, such as deductions for insulation, double glazing, and other socially desirable improvements, might also be devolved and could give a real boost to local housing policy debate.

Inference no. 3
Locally devolved taxes must be designed to enhance local decision-making, the local economy and local democracy, or they make no sense at all.

Right now the UK's policy on tax devolution is, unfortunately, in that category of making no sense at all.

This then suggests a fourth area of policy concern. As already noted, tax has a macroeconomic function and this is related to management of the national economy as a whole. This objective cannot be forgotten even if the devolution of taxing powers takes place, and, that being the case, regional and local governments will have to exercise their powers within an overall framework that they must agree to, but which may eventually require arbitration procedures in the event of dispute.

That framework would have to suggest how much tax was expected to be raised from the local economy for which each regional or local government was responsible, taking into account both the macro-economic position and the national government target on redistribution of income and wealth into or out of the area in question. This issue is essential: there is no country that enjoys anything like an equal geographic distribution of either income or wealth, and that inequality must not be exacerbated by the creation of devolved taxing powers. To protect against this, the principle of cross-subsidization that has long been inherent in the UK economy (but which the current government is threatening to modify in the cases of Northern Ireland and Scotland) has to be preserved and even reinforced within the framework of devolved powers.

The object for doing so should be obvious: it is about ensuring that those devolved layers of government do really concentrate on managing their economies and do not, like tax havens, use their powers to undermine the right of other regions to collect the tax owing to them. The aim of devolution is better government, not worse, after all. That can only be achieved within agreed policy frameworks.

Inference no. 4
Devolved taxes must operate within an agreed national framework of macroeconomic management.

Having established these goals it is next essential to look at the more detailed levels of policy coherence that will, inevitably, fall largely to central government. What is undoubtedly true is that at present our tax system is riddled with policy incoherence. Take, as example, one of our more anachronistic taxes, national insurance. This tax was designed in the Second World War for a post-war era where long-term, secure employment was envisaged for the vast majority of people, with only a small minority being considered likely to be in self-employment and the use of limited companies by those self-employed people being presumed to be rare. As a result this tax was designed in two parts: one charged on the employee and the other on the employer. The aim was threefold. First, national insurance was meant to fund the new National Health Service. Second, it was meant to fund new, much enhanced pensions, at a time when many people did not live for long beyond the designated retirement age of sixty-five,[1] and thirdly, the national insurance contributions a person made determined their entitlement to many in-work (or rather, out-of-work) benefits, from which the self-employed were excluded, which is why they paid much lower rates of contribution.

This was a great tax at the time. There was policy coherence throughout its design and by using the then new Pay As You Earn system it was easy to collect, as the vast majority of people in the country had one job, and many of them stayed with the same employer for many years. What could go wrong?

The economy changed; that's what happened. We now have five million self-employed people and, as importantly, large numbers of people in multiple employments that they change frequently (with some periods on benefits in between those employments, on occasion). In addition the cost of the NHS, let alone pensions and other benefits, has far outstripped the national contributions now made that are supposed to pay for them, as life expectancies, living standards and the complexity of medicine have all advanced. The result is that national insurance as now charged makes no sense at all in the modern economy of work.

It does not make sense in some other ways either. First, hundreds of thousands of self-employed people now form companies to reward themselves for their work by way of dividend payments, which do not attract a national insurance charge. As a result national insurance charging is now riddled with loopholes: the design of this charge and the availability of limited liability entities at incredibly low cost has permitted, in combination, what is, in effect, massive tax abuse.

Second, when there is now an employment crisis in the UK, whether it relates to low pay, youth unemployment, under-employment or zero hours contracts, charging national insurance on jobs in a way that suppresses wages and at the same time adds to employer cost makes no sense at all. There is no economic logic left to the tax.

And the contributory principle has almost gone. It is true that to get a full old-age pension thirty years of contributions have to be paid, but the fact is that those not well off who do not qualify on the basis of their national insurance contributions rightly get other benefits to make up the shortfall. The whole tax has become anomalous.

Inference no. 5

The tax system has to be under continuous review to make sure it is not past its sell-by date. Those taxes that no longer make sense have to be replaced if the tax system is not to undermine economic objectives.

What is clear is that unless such reviews happen perverse consequences will follow: national insurance may have been well designed for a purpose but that has long gone and the result may now be as counter-productive as once it was advantageous. Tax design is not neutral, and whilst a tax may be good at reclaiming money from the economy (and national insurance is, contributing over £100 billion a year to the UK Treasury), that does not mean that it is efficient.

Inference no. 6
Money raising and tax efficiency are not the same thing.

It follows then that tax must be integrated into the social policies of government and the tax decisions a government makes should always be viewed through the lens of their social policy consequences. How to achieve this goal is considered in more depth in the next chapter. Examples of areas where alignment might be required are the focus of attention here.

There are obvious policy issues where this interaction between tax and policy is essential. These include:

- Growth
- Employment
- Innovation and enterprise
- Banking
- Benefits and pensions
- Education
- Housing
- Environment

Others could be selected; these are sufficient to prove the point. It is important to note, though, that some areas where policy coherence is required are generic, and others relate to scale. So, for example, the relationship between tax and growth is fundamentally an issue of scale. Government activity is a key contributor to measures of growth, since government spending and investment play a significant part in the various elements that make up national income; but unless that activity is on a large enough scale it won't have the necessary impact on the economy as a whole when government intervention is required. If the market fails to deliver stable growth (as it usually does fail) it needs to be counterbalanced by government intervening to either inject or withdraw money, in order to ensure stability is maintained. So, if consistent growth is to be achieved, government spending, and so the extent of government activity, simply has to be big enough to ensure that its intervention will be noticed.

There is another dimension to this issue of scale: precisely because the government has to be able to withdraw from the economy on occasion (when the market is booming beyond capacity) then, by definition, it is impossible for the government to restrict its activity to the barest minimum that represents the basic obligation it must fulfil if the state and its people are to survive, because none of that could then be withdrawn if macroeconomic management demanded it. In other words, and as a matter of fact, the state must in normal times be undertaking activity that is discretionary, and on occasion even activity that could be undertaken by the market, because if that is not the case then government discretion in economic management is lost, and the objective of achieving stable growth goes with it.

An example might make the point. The government has some activities that it undertakes because it thinks them desirable although they are not essential. The Olympic Games was one; quite a lot of business support might be another. If there were an economic boom it would be entirely reasonable to withdraw from such activity precisely because it would not then be needed or because the private sector could fund it itself. But unless the option of withdrawing from such activity is available without harm arising then the macroeconomic management flexibility that is essential to restore balance when an economy is overheating would not be available to the government.

How does this impact taxation? Simply by saying that the tax system cannot be minimized so that it has minimum impact on the market.

Inference no. 7
The tax system is intended to have an economic impact and so must be big enough to deliver it.

Big taxes – income tax, VAT, corporation taxes, excise duties and right now national insurance – do then have to be in the tax system in some way or other. Without them, or similar taxes, the tax system is just not big enough to work. That may appear to be a circular argument, but once you accept that tax is about more than raising money it is also a necessary one.

Let's be clear though: growth as recorded by GDP is not the same as delivering full employment. Growth comes from a variety of sources, including rents, profits, speculation and even from growing asset prices, such as those of residential property. And some very significant areas of growth, like the rise in financial services over the last decades, have been increasingly marked by large sales and profits from a declining number of employees. So having a state sector large enough to handle market volatility in order to deliver continuing growth is not enough. That growth has to be shared with people whose main opportunity to participate in the benefits of growth is through work.

So how does the tax system create work beyond those 55,000 or so people currently employed by HMRC? As already noted, right now it does not. Because national insurance charges employers tax for having employees it does the exact opposite of what is intended in this regard. Perversely, and at a time when there is a savings glut in the world[2] and there is no need whatsoever to encourage yet more money to be put aside in the economy for no productive purpose (because the level of investment is in no way dependent upon the level of savings in an economy, as the discussion in Chapter 4 on the way money is created has shown), the net effect of this bias is to massively overtax labour, which needs to be put to work on decent wages when too many people in the UK are currently paid too little and too many people have low-productivity jobs. The tax system reinforces both these undesirable trends by creating marginal tax rates that, when seen from an employer's perspective, can amount to about 45.8 per cent of the total stated salary cost of employing a person at the UK median wage of around £26,000 a year. This is made up of 20 per cent income tax plus combined employer's and employee's national insurance of 25.8 per cent of stated gross pay at this level of income. In contrast the marginal tax rate paid on unearned income of a similar amount is very unlikely to exceed 20 per cent, and could actually be less depending upon its source. When it is more employment and not more savings that the UK needs, the UK tax system is working hard to achieve the exact opposite outcome, judging by the signals of desirable activity that it is sending to the economy.

This can happen in the other areas noted as well. So, for example, with regard to small business, tax policy should encourage risk-taking and investment, prevent unfair competition and ensure that effective succession planning is possible. These are key business objectives. However, at present it does instead encourage the diversion of effort into tax planning and avoidance because the tax rates on self-employment and the tax payable by companies on broadly similar income can be significantly different. Above fairly low levels of earnings there is almost always a significant advantage to incorporating a business for tax purposes, and that distortion makes no sense for most businesses, not least because it adds to the supposed burdens of admin that is meant to harm business effectiveness.

In addition, for those who are both employed and self-employed (as is increasingly common) the tax system could actually encourage portfolio working. But it does not. The PAYE system, which was so effective in 1945, is now so rigid that it forces people into either false self-employments or to moonlight, such is the complexity of getting tax right within the system. This makes no sense at all.

As it also makes no sense that, when high marginal tax rates are held to be such a disincentive to work, those who have been to university and consequently have taken out student loans have 9 per cent of their earnings above a relatively low threshold deducted in loan repayments – a tax for all practical purposes – on top of income tax and national insurance. When you add it all together it is actually possible for a graduate on £25,000 a year to have tax and loan deductions of 41 per cent showing on their pay slip, and an effective tax rate, including employer's national insurance that reduces their real pay, of approximately 50 per cent. When this rate is widely argued to be a disincentive to work for those earning more than £150,000 a year in the UK it is perverse that it is readily applied to large numbers of those earning around median pay in this country. Either the rhetoric or the policy is wrong in this case.

It is also perverse that the tax system interacts with the benefits system so badly (and will still do so after the introduction of universal credit) that marginal tax rates of up to 80 per cent are possible over small, but significant, ranges of income as people move off benefits and into work: as they start paying tax and national insurance but lose support from the state as a result.

Banking is another area where tax and policy conflict. Since 2008 many politicians have argued we need to diversify the UK economy away from financial services, but those same services are at the same time under-taxed. Not only does the UK have a wide range of its own tax havens available so that banks can hide their profits offshore, it also does not charge VAT on financial services and so relatively underprices banking activity as if it were an essential service like healthcare and education, and that makes no sense at all.

The pension system too, after changes from George Osborne, lacks any tax logic. For many years it was the case that when an individual or employer made a contribution to a private pension they very clearly reduced an obligation on the state to provide a pension, so tax reliefs (and, on occasion, national insurance reliefs) on pension contributions made sense. But over time the logic of this relief has been eroded. Pensions are now becoming little more than another form of saving for those better off. The provision of tax relief to encourage savings that the economy does not need and which, in the vast majority of cases, simply increase the wealth divide (because only those already sufficiently well off to make ends meet can, in the main, make pension savings) makes little sense, and yet such reliefs cost the UK Exchequer more than £48 billion a year.[3]

Nor is there any sense in other tax-related encouragements for saving which have no link to what the saved funds are used for, such as ISAs. They would only have a point if used to promote local investment, social projects or environmental projects, all of which are underfunded.

This is also true of a plethora of investment-related tax incentive schemes that are, in reality, little more than tax shelters. The social benefit arising from the sums expended, effectively to subsidize these schemes, for social purposes that are rarely adequately defined, is almost invariably unquantified, so that the real cost to society, and those less well off within it, cannot be understood.

The illogicality extends to housing. We have excepted people's homes from capital gains tax. Meanwhile, to an extent seen in few other societies, the UK has suffered from house price inflation as people have been willing to overpay for houses knowing that the shortage of housing supply and the favourable tax treatment it has enjoyed have made houses an ideal form of wealth preservation however irrational the resulting allocation of the housing stock, or wealth within it, might be. This problem is only exacerbated by the differing tax treatment of buy-to-let and buy-to-live-in housing. Buy-to-let housing, usually purchased by those who already have a home and some wealth and which is intended to provide an investment return, is given tax relief on the cost of sums borrowed to fund the acquisition, but buy-to-live-in property does not enjoy similar treatment. As a result, speculative property is, to a large degree, paid for out of pre-tax income but housing for those who really need it is paid for out of post-tax income. The illogicality is obvious.

The same is true with regard to the environment. We tax least the most carbon-emitting form of transport, which is air travel. We also encourage the carriage around the world of goods that could easily be produced locally, by not taxing the extremely dirty bunker fuel of the world's largest ships. And almost invariably the tax system demands no return at all to the resource that is scarcest of all in our world – the planet itself. That payment of a return to the planet is, however, possible. If only we taxed excessive consumption we would, without doubt, create funds for future generations who will have to manage the legacy of our mistakes, such as nuclear waste. We could also fund investment in the alternative technologies that we collectively need. That, however, requires new forms of tax altogether. They are possible. But they have to be designed around policy coherence and goal congruence.

As the example of national insurance demonstrates, we did do that at one time. And now we don't. What we cannot, unfortunately, do is move in one go from where we are now to where we need to be. Tax systems cannot handle that degree of disruption. But nor can change work if we do not know where we might need to go. So, based on the principles already set out in this book, the next chapter discusses what some characteristics of an ideal tax system might look like before, in the final chapter, I suggest how we might move towards that goal from where we are now.

8

The ideal tax system

The essential quality of the taxes that we need is that they must work. It's worth recalling what that means. Taxes must do six things, which were noted in Chapter 3. They have to:

1. Reclaim money the government has spent into the economy for re-use
2. Ratify the value of money
3. Reorganize the economy
4. Redistribute income and wealth
5. Reprice goods and services
6. Raise representation

And, as noted in Chapter 6, they have to be built on the foundations of:

1. Peace
2. Equality
3. Truth, and
4. Simplicity

That being the case it is important to understand just what it is that makes an ideal tax system.

First, it must be possible to define what is being taxed. This is called the tax base.

Second, it must be possible to locate that tax base. Quite literally, that means it must be possible to find it.

Thirdly, having found it then it must also be possible to quantify that base in ways that do not attract too much dispute. Some taxes are more prone to such valuation problems than others.

And even then, fourthly, there is the small matter of working out who actually owns the tax base. After all, issuing a tax bill to an unknown person does not increase the chance of it being paid.

Finally, there is the issue of doing all these things accountably or a government will quickly lose public confidence in the justice of what it is seeking to do. This chapter considers these issues.

Defining the tax base is a much more complex process than most people, tax experts and economists included, think it to be. Most of them use relatively trite descriptions for the taxes we now have. So, for example, they split taxes between direct taxes (on income, capital gains and profits) and indirect taxes (on sales, consumption and use of facilities). And they use terms such as sales and profits, as I have just done, to describe the tax bases. This, however, will not do. Tax bases need much more consideration than these mere descriptions imply if confusion about how taxes and tax systems work is to be avoided.

The important word in the last paragraph is 'systems'. For too long this word has been forgotten and so individual taxes are discussed in isolation. This is a mistake. Our taxes should not exist in isolation from each other: they exist to suit overall goals and they must be appraised in that case on the contribution each tax can make to achieving those collective goals.

What helps make this possible is the realization that all our taxes share some quite strong common themes. In particular, although it is hardly ever said, they do in practice almost entirely relate to the taxation of wealth. This is hardly surprising: tax is (as I have argued) intimately related to money. Because tax is about reclaiming the money the government has spent into existence, possessing money is a necessary precondition to paying tax. And since money is our most common measure of wealth, the link between tax and wealth is not hard to establish. Despite this it does, however, need explanation.

The first linkage between tax and wealth is to be

found in many of our most widely known taxes, such as income tax, corporation tax and capital gains tax. These are, in fact, all taxes on the accumulation of wealth. That is because income, if properly defined, records the increase in our wealth over a period of time before taking into account the spending we incur to maintain ourselves.

A wide range of activities can contribute to that increase in wealth. Most of us will think of income from work, whether from a wage or the profit from a business activity, as the primary source of that increase, but in practice these are far from being the only sources of this wealth accumulation over time. Cash received from rents, investment income, the sale of our own property at a profit, and the receipt of gifts can all increase our cash wealth. Historically many of these have been treated differently for tax purposes but the reality is that as far as anyone is concerned (and I stress, *anyone*) £1 from one source of accumulated wealth is identical in economic value to £1 from any other source. In fact, when put side by side as coins, or when mixed together in a bank account, it would be impossible for a person to tell whether a particular £1 was from earned income resulting from work, or from savings income (such as interest on a bank account), or from a capital gain on the sale of shares or a house, or a gift from another person. A pound is a pound is a pound and each contributes in the same way to a person's well-being, albeit (as already noted) the more of such pounds that there are the less each one is individually significant to the person who owns them (which is why progressive taxation not only makes sense, but is economically necessary).

This idea of wealth accumulation has broader applications. So, for example, some forms of wealth accumulation are only possible because of licences granted by the state. Examples include income from royalties on patents and copyrights: these would not exist without state support. In such cases the idea that all income is to be treated equally for tax breaks down: specific extra charges might be justified by the type of structure from which the income is earned and the extent to which the state is required to help create the legal form and maintain the contractual claim to that income stream. This might apply to the income a person earns from companies and trusts, or from royalties.

This logic has particular relevance in the case of banks who can, as has already been noted in this book, create money out of thin air because they have been granted a banking licence, and can then charge interest on the funds that they have created costlessly. The gain in this case is technically called seigniorage, which is usually defined as the profit made by a government by issuing currency. Banking licences actively outsource this right to make profit: additional taxes on banks seek to recover the additional wealth that they have accumulated as a result.

In combination these observations make an important point: what they imply is that some of the preferential tax regimes that have existed, for example for capital gains, which have attracted additional tax allowances for the people that enjoy them and have often been taxed at lower rates than are charged on income, make no economic sense. Capital gains, once the original cost of acquiring whatever is sold has been taken into account, should logically be taxed in exactly the same way as any other source of income, and be added into the individual's total income for the purposes of calculating the appropriate tax rate to charge. The only Chancellor to ever get this right in the UK was, slightly oddly, Nigel Lawson.

One knotty question arises from treating capital gains as income in this way which is whether inflation should be ignored in calculating the amount of gain made on the sale. In a time of high inflation to ignore its effects would produce an unjust outcome: people would be taxed not on their increase in wealth, but on the falling value of money. There have been periods, such as the 1970s and 1980s in the UK, when this was a real issue and steps had to be taken to prevent this injustice. When, however, inflation is consistently low, as it has generally been in the UK for some time now, simplicity demands that inflation be ignored for tax purposes.

Perhaps even more controversially, the idea that all increases in wealth are, as a matter of principle, similar for taxation purposes implies that what a person receives as a gift should be subject to tax in the same way as their income. This is, of course, completely contrary to current UK taxation practice, where people making gifts on death, or in the seven years before it, are subject to tax on the amount given away but the recipients are not charged tax. That is the way that Inheritance Tax works, and it is deeply unpopular as a consequence. That is actually unsurprising: economically the tax is completely inconsistent with any other tax base the UK uses, and people may sense its illogicality.

But what should be put in its place? If, as is obviously true, gifts increase a person's wealth, it appears unjust that they be tax-free when the increase in wealth resulting from work is taxed. Pragmatically, however, there are problems: for instance every parent provides for their children in ways that might be described as gifts which nobody would want to tax, not least because those gifts do, almost certainly, come out of the donor's income and not their accumulated wealth. A tax on the receipt of gifts, desirable as it might be, does therefore need mechanisms to ensure that it only charges real transfers of wealth from one person to another. If that could be done the logic of adding such receipts to income, with, perhaps, a mechanism to apply a tax rate averaged over a number of years, would seem fair.

That stance does then imply that wealth is, in itself, taxable, and I would argue that it is. If, after all, one of the main objectives of tax is to redistribute income and wealth it makes no sense to ignore wealth as a tax base, either in its own right, or as a source of income that does, in turn, require redistribution. A wealth tax is, then, an essential part of a tax system even if capital gains and gifts made out of wealth are already taxed elsewhere. The rate at which wealth tax might be charged may well be modest, and it is clear that exemptions would be required for the necessary cost of providing a home (but not of landed estates) and for reasonable sums put aside to provide for old age, but above and beyond that the arguments against a wealth tax have always been pragmatic and not theoretical. When, as until very recently, it was so easy to relocate wealth out of the country and into a tax haven and so avoid any liability, wealth taxes looked something like honesty box arrangements, which cannot be thought an equitable outcome. In the new era now being created, of automatic information exchange of data on people who hold accounts and own companies and trusts in tax havens, this pragmatic objection can be consigned to history. The tireless campaigning of the tax justice movement to achieve this goal has made wealth taxation possible.

The argument that wealth taxes should not be imposed upon business assets can be dismissed. Pragmatically, 95 per cent of all businesses are likely to fall below any threshold at which a wealth tax will be charged: the small enterprise economy will never be impacted by a wealth tax. Once a business is on a scale that passes that threshold there are good reasons for charging tax on the owners of the wealth implicit in them. Such businesses will, almost invariably, make use of limited liability, and since this is a privilege granted by society it should be paid for. If the wealth of those who own businesses is protected from unforeseen loss, which is the case when a limited liability company is used, then a premium is due for that benefit. Next, although many business owners like to claim to the contrary, no business is built solely on personal endeavour; it is always the case that the state contributes substantially to its success, either by simply providing the legal framework in which it can operate, or by protecting its assets from claim from third parties, or by providing the legal infrastructure in which it can trade, or by training its key personnel during their school and university education as well as ensuring that they come to work by and large fit and well each day. A return is due for these benefits.

A wealth tax on business assets would be consistent with the objective of redistribution (and concentration of wealth is rarely beneficial to society), but at the same time it might actually bring benefit to the business. Settlement of the tax could be made in kind, through the annual transfer of ownership of small parts of the business to a trust arranged in such a way as to ensure that employees in the business can be represented upon its board, have access to information that they need, and ultimately have a say in its long-term future. By providing talented employees with the right to participate in the business's conduct, that tax can diversify the pool of talent available to a business upon which to depend for its future success.

Another type of wealth I think it essential to tax is that implicit in the ownership of land. For too long land ownership in the UK has been too concentrated. Too much of its ownership is unrecorded; or, when such records are kept, the beneficial ownership may be disguised through the use of offshore limited companies. As a result land speculation has sometimes been hard to identify, and therefore to tax. Meanwhile preferential tax regimes for personal homes have resulted in house price increases out of all proportion to income inflation, so that very many people in the UK, the young in particular, are now excluded from the housing market. At the same time, local authority taxation, which is largely based upon the outdated valuation of properties (a crude tax, created in a hurry to replace the hated poll tax), has become deeply dysfunctional for that reason. As a consequence land value taxation has now become essential.

Land value taxation should apply to all land value, without exception, where the land value is the amount for which the land could be let without having been developed. The land value tax due on an empty plot would therefore be the same as that due on the house next door. As already noted, this is an ideal tax to be managed by a devolved authority or regional government. The charge would be made on the owner, and not on the occupier of the land. In other words, this is a tax paid by landlords and the owner-occupiers of land. This means it is quite clear what it is: it is a tax on wealth.

There are five advantages to land value taxation. First, it cannot really be avoided: if the tax is not paid the land is forfeited. Second, it encourages the productive use of land because the charge is made whether or not the land is in use. Third, it allows the taxing authority to achieve environmental policy goals through active engagement with that land use, for example by using allowances and exemptions. Fourth, this tax shifts the burden from those who are less able to pay it – that is tenants – to those who always can, who are landlords. As a result this tax tends to be progressive in its nature, which most other land-based taxes ever charged in countries like the UK have never been, and which the UK council tax is very definitely not. Finally, because land use tends to improve when land value tax is in use yields rise, there are economic gains as a result and reduced social cost from vacant land and so the system provides net economic gains beyond revenue raised.

This consideration of direct charges on wealth does not, however, bring to a close the consideration of wealth taxation. Transfers of wealth provide another basis for tax. The sale of goods is one such transfer: when a sale takes place wealth is transferred between the participants. Sales taxes and value-added taxes can very clearly be applied to these transfers. The UK has had a VAT since 1973.

Trading in other assets can also be taxed in this way. So, for example, stamp duty has been charged upon the sale of shares and land in the UK for a long time.

It does not take much extension of that logic to come to a financial transaction tax chargeable upon the purchase and sale of a wide range of financial instruments and upon speculation in money itself, including foreign exchange. Such a tax has been widely resisted by the City of London – and by the UK government as a consequence – but in practice the present situation, where some financial transactions are taxed at a relatively high rate (as happens in the case of share dealings) while others fall outside the scope of that tax (as do many forms of financial derivative trading, even if the derivative relates to shares), creates tax loopholes, and a horizontal inequality in the financial services market.

The case for a financial transactions tax is overwhelmingly strong. For a start, it is a tax that can be applied to banks, unlike a VAT (which for technical reasons is almost impossible to apply in their case). And since it is deliberately designed to discourage trading activity it could also be a useful tool for intervention in the market. Very few people outside the financial services sector now doubt that the high volume of financial transactions being undertaken is, in itself, a destabilizing factor in the world economy; by reducing that volume a financial transactions tax can correct a market failure. Moreover, if the rate of this tax is variable, increasing in line with the number of transactions being undertaken (and this is technically possible), it will make trading increasingly unattractive at times when markets are panicking, which is precisely when they need to be slowed down. Such a tax could, in that case, be an essential protection against market failure caused by panic.

Taking the idea of a financial transactions tax just a little further there is, in fact, no reason at all why money transfers should not be taxable. It is entirely possible to tax all transactions through bank accounts that a person or company operates (transfers between accounts under common control, which banks could easily identify, could be excluded). This charge could be applied to the aggregate of all deposits or withdrawals from accounts, or both (which may be necessary, else the incentive to relocate accounts outside the UK for trading purposes might be very high: taxing both sides of the transaction ensures that at least part of any arrangement impacting the UK will always be collected).

As with a financial transactions tax on share and derivative trading such a tax would be challenged by the powerful forces of the banking sector, and yet it has been proved to work: from 1993 to 2007 Brazil had such a tax charge on all bank accounts at the rate of 0.38 per cent on almost all transactions, during which period this tax provided much of the funding for its healthcare system. It was disputes on whether there should be such funding rather than whether the tax worked that resulted in its demise.[1] Australia has also used such a tax, but no longer does so.

To have such a tax in the UK would be pioneering, but there is good reason for considering it, in particular as a replacement for national insurance. National insurance has always been a UK tax that has fallen outside the logic of having a relationship to wealth. Instead it is a tax where the payment supposedly represents a charge, with the clue being in the name: there was meant to be an insurance element in this contribution when it was first created. This insurance component has long gone: the contributory principle has disappeared from many benefits that are now paid; national insurance contributions do not now pay for the NHS; and pensions are not paid on an insurance basis but are instead paid on a current-year basis, i.e. current contributions pay for current pensions and there is, as a result, no guarantee of a state pension upon retirement even if a person has paid national insurance throughout their working career. This is, then, a dishonest tax that is no longer fit for purpose: no one should be taxed on the basis of a charge for a service that it cannot be guaranteed will be supplied. What is more, since it falls solely on labour and not on capital this tax creates massive distortions in our tax system, suppresses real wages and encourages large amounts of tax abuse.

National insurance also raises well over £100 billion a year for the UK Exchequer. Replacing such a tax will take time, and care, and merging it into income tax is not realistic, even if it sounds superficially appealing: the resulting required tax rates will be too high. In addition, we need a tax where the tax base is primarily on consumption, but where the likely outcome is progressive, and not regressive as VAT is. This is for social reasons, but also to discourage excessive consumption in a world where carbon usage has to be reduced. This is why I think that a progressive tax on the total sum paid into and out of people's and companies' bank accounts is now essential. This simply requires that the rate charged increases as the total payments into and out of bank accounts connected to a person increase. What that rate might be would be open to debate and the transition from national insurance could be gradual: we are talking about a major new tax here, after all. That said, the reality is that this charge on bank transactions could be the best approximation to a progressive carbon usage tax (CUT) that is likely to be available. And because this charge can be applied to businesses and individuals alike, this is the tax that can, in the twenty-first century, end the absurd need to tax labour and its wealth creation and instead shift that tax to excessive consumption, a shift we know is now needed.

Business would not be excluded from this charge's progressive nature. Whilst I would suggest that this tax should be imposed at flat rates on business, this rate could vary for each business activity whilst smaller business could be exempt. There would, of course, have to be quite powerful penalties for those seeking to avoid this charge by moving offshore – with the penalty being levied through income and corporation taxes. And, if all that could be achieved, I suggest we might have the tax Thomas Piketty was seeking when he said he was looking for a global wealth tax.

All of which does not mean that we have finished with the taxation of wealth as yet. Abusing the collective wealth of others is another basis for charging tax. This is, of course, the reason why some taxes on what economists call externalities are levied. So, for example, taxes on carbon and other forms of pollution are charged because the emission of noxious substances imposes costs, both now and, through climate change, in the future.

A similar externality that has potential impact upon the collective wealth of others is created when trading takes place through limited liability companies. If these fail the cost of their doing so falls in part on their creditors and sometimes more widely onto society at large, as the banking crisis of 2008 proved. Income recorded in a limited liability company should, as a result, be subject to higher rates of tax than are charged on income recorded in other ways.

This logic of taxing generic externalities to correct market failures is not, however, the rationale for all charges of this type: taxes on tobacco, alcohol and road use do not fit within this framework. In these cases the taxes are meant to be a contribution towards the cost that the user imposes upon society by their behaviour. This is a blatant charging exercise. National insurance is another tax supposedly of this type but its relationship with the benefits system is now so eroded that its demise is now required, as already noted.

Mention of benefits does however link to another aspect of wealth taxation. This arises because a social security system is, in effect, a form of negative wealth taxation. When it is determined that a person's likely level of essential spending will, in all probability, be more than the wealth accumulation that they can enjoy in a given period, for whatever reason and from whatever source, then an effective social security system must step in to make sure that the person does not slip into poverty, which in this context is not just an absence of wealth, but a need to have access to it.

Any system of social security (or benefits, or welfare) will always interact with the tax system, and for decades it has been acknowledged that countries that run the two mainly or entirely independently of each other can create significant and perverse consequences. This is

Figure 10: Required minimum income payments for proposed citizen's income

Family type	Minimum Income Standard – (£/week)
Single, no children	192.59
Couple, no children	301.74
Lone parent, 1 child	275.59
Lone parent, 2 children	361.99
Lone parent, 3 children	457.66
Couple, 1 child	374.17
Couple, 2 children	454.52
Couple, 3 children	554.55
Couple, 4 children	605.80
Single, pensioner	158.74
Couple, pensioner	231.48

Source: www.minimumincomestandard.org/2012_update.htm

especially true of the way benefits are withdrawn as a person's earnings rise. The combined effect of the two processes has created marginal tax rates in excess of 80 per cent of income in the UK for those on well below average incomes.[2] In an ideal system this issue would be resolved by integrating the tax and social security systems. The best way to achieve this is firstly by paying a citizen's income to everyone in the country, irrespective of whether they work or not, and secondly by changing the income tax system to reflect that fact (having assumed the tax on bank account usage, noted above, could already accommodate the national insurance changes).

If there were a citizen's income the right would be universal. It would, for example, go to children as well as adults, even if at reduced rate. Economist Howard Reed and I modelled such a system in 2013.[3] The required minimum income payments we assumed necessary to ensure that all children were out of relative poverty (60 per cent of median income) at the time we did the work were as shown in Figure 10 on the previous page. I stress, these sums would, in the system we modelled, be paid without question: they represent an entitlement. As a result they would, however, replace almost all benefits barring some housing benefit where rents are particularly high, and some disability benefits. They would also replace the old age pension, and, it should be noted, were higher than those pensions paid at that time (and at the time of writing).

As is clear from this table a couple with, for example, four children would get an allowance of £31,500 a year, tax free, under this system. The other side of the coin would, however, be higher taxes. To ensure that this was both possible and suitably progressive we envisaged a small tax-free personal allowance of maybe £2,000 or so (but remember everyone gets the tax-free payment noted above as a massive compensation for this change) followed by a 25 per cent tax band and then a main 50 per cent band. At the other end of the income scale, incomes above £100,000 would pay tax at higher rates ranging from 60 per cent to a maximum of 70 per cent for incomes above £150,000. This might sound high but the figures were influenced by the need to include national insurance in the charge. If a charge on bank transactions was instead put in place, as I now suggest is desirable, then they could be reduced somewhat. We called this arrangement a Unified Income Tax system and it was our belief that it could quite cost-effectively replace the existing UK national insurance, income tax and benefits systems and balance out in its costings.

These reforms have five key advantages. First, the basic or citizen's income to be paid would mean the effective eradication of poverty (on the 'below 60 per cent of median income' definition). Second, marginal tax rates for families on low incomes are much lower under this system than any conceivable where separate tax and benefits systems are operated, with a maximum of about 60 per cent for those in receipt of housing support and 45 per cent for those not on housing support. The disincentive to work that is such a strong feature of the existing benefits system would, therefore, disappear. Third, the whole tax and benefits system would be hugely simplified, with only one direct tax and three benefits – the universal citizen's income and a means-tested benefit to assist with housing costs plus another to address significant disability. This would, for example, mean the end of the whole national insurance system. Fourth, everyone would get the benefits to which they were entitled under this system – a major issue in the present system where it is believed that more than £15 billion a year of benefits are unclaimed.[4] And finally, by paying benefits to everyone without exception the stigma of the benefits system is removed.

The question many would ask of this proposal is whether people would still choose to work if they had a basic income. Some may not, of course, but the truth is that work is much more than an economic activity. Work is a social activity. It does, for many people, provide purpose. And for many people it is also about fulfilling their potential. There is also the fact that under this system work always pays, whilst the freedom to choose that this system would create would mean that the pressure on employers to provide high-quality work, with training and flexibility, would be enormous, which is exactly what the UK economy needs if it is to create the productivity that is so lacking. We believed, and I still believe, that the risk of many falling out of work as a result of this payment would be small.

Wealth, its accumulation, ownership, transfer and absence, as well as the external threats that some behaviour might pose to it, can explain the vast majority of the taxes, and benefits, that any society needs (excluding those taxes that are, in effect, insurance-based charges). This does not, however, suggest how these tax bases are to then be identified, estimated as to value and charged to tax. This is not the place for a detailed explanation of how this needs to be done in the case of each tax: the reality is that much of this is already known. Some general rules and explanation as to how some major exceptions might be dealt with – which is where many of the problems have arisen – will have to suffice.

Starting with the basis on which the charge to tax is to be defined, what is vital is that this be as broadly specified as possible. As already explained in this book, the UK approach to charging tax has been to define what is subject to tax and whatever is not mentioned is then assumed to be not taxable. This has been the foundation of most tax abuse in the UK: trying to find the loopholes that have kept a transaction out of tax has become the tax avoider's art. The solution is obvious: all of the potential tax base must, in an ideal tax system, be considered taxable unless it is specifically excepted from charge. The importance of doing this can hardly be stressed enough: as experience has shown, there are enormous limitations to language when it comes to defining tax bases. An approach in which 'all is in the tax base unless specifically ruled out' is essential in that case.

This approach must also be mirrored when defining what may be permitted to reduce a tax bill. In essence the answer is in this case as simple: nothing should be allowed as an offset against income unless it is specifically permitted in law. So, for example, the fact that an expense is in a set of business accounts should not mean that tax relief is available upon it: only those expenses definitely prescribed as permissible must be subject to that relief. Generally speaking tax systems have been better in defining this side of the equation to date even if some permitted expenses are open to debate as to the usefulness of the relief given. Many tax reliefs given for interest paid, for example, are subject to this doubt.

All this legislation then needs to be backed up by a purposive approach to new tax laws, in turn supported by a general anti-avoidance principle in UK tax law. The reasons for both of these have already been explained in this book: the effect is to say that if anyone tries to artificially get round the law to secure a tax saving then the steps they have taken to achieve this goal will be ignored when it comes to assessing them to tax. Nothing could be fairer, more straightforward or certain than that. Everyone knows exactly where they stand.

This approach should also apply to those issues that arise when trying to find the tax base. The powers needed to secure information on who has what taxable transactions within the UK will be discussed later in this chapter: the challenge needing to be addressed first is to what extent transactions located outside the UK need to be brought within the scope of UK taxation. The answer to this question is, thankfully, straightforward. The most massive loopholes would be opened up in UK tax law if a person could avoid their responsibility to pay tax in this country simply by moving a source of income, or an asset, or bank account (or whatever else they might seek to move) outside the UK. In that case a UK-resident person has to be taxable in full on their worldwide income (including gains and receipt of gifts) as well as on their worldwide wealth and bank accounts. Unless this is done, horizontal equity is impossible, as it would also be if some people were outside the scope of this rule for any reason. Whilst it is fair that those seeking temporary residence in the UK (four years, or less) might, for reasons of administrative ease and international equity, be taxable only on their UK income and what-ever of their worldwide income is brought to the UK during that period, after that time has elapsed it is vital that they must be taxed on their total worldwide income. The UK's domicile rule has to be consigned to the bin of history.

The same rule must also be applied to UK companies. The possibility that a UK company might seek to avoid tax by artificially relocating activity into a company taxed in another country is unacceptable. This is, admittedly, a complex issue that is also related to how to tax people equitably on the income they record in limited liability companies, but a solution has to be found or tax abuse is inevitable. Thankfully an answer is available. In principle all income from which a UK person might benefit that is earned abroad, whether in a company or not, must first be subject to the tax laws of the state where it is earned. After that, and if there is additional tax to pay, it must be subject to UK tax with credit given for taxes already paid. If earned in a person's own name this should happen in the year in which the income arises. If it is in a company there may be technical reasons why that is not possible until the time it is brought into the UK (although note the suggestion I make below on small company tax, which could overcome this problem in their case). And to make sure that income is properly allocated to each country in which a group of companies operated, its total group tax profits should be allocated to states using a formula that seeks to establish just where its real economic activities are located. Significant factors are likely to be where its staff are, where its sales are from and to, where it extracts minerals (if that is part of its business) and, maybe, where its assets are located. This system of apportionment is not perfect but right now there are few people with any knowledge of tax, bar the tax avoidance industry and its clients, who think that the taxation of international companies works at present. In that case reform is well overdue, and the arrangement I propose is vastly better and would be subject to significantly less abuse than the existing one where all companies are treated as if they are independent of each other. That assumption is, of course, factually incorrect and the result is that the current system of international tax of companies is based on what might, politely, be called 'make believe'. I am suggesting it be based on economic facts.

Reform is also needed when it comes to calculating business profits. Accounts are largely unsuitable for this purpose. The International Financial Reporting Standards Foundation, which sets the rules for most large company accounts, actually makes this clear: it has admitted that the data reported using its standards are not suited to this purpose. However, since it is impossible to expect companies and businesses to keep two sets of books – one for the members and another for the tax authorities – it is now clear that active cooperation between governments is needed to ensure that the correct data required to assess business income for tax are available in future. This might well involve agreeing what information they should require be added to the standards set by the International Financial Reporting Standards Foundation to achieve this goal. They might also explore whether simplifications are possible for tax: one simplification that would suit those businesses that have to invest heavily to undertake their trades would be to permit the offset of all expenditure on new equipment in the year it was incurred. This would counter a bias in existing tax rules that tends to favour speculators and banks over companies engaged in more useful economic activity.

There are further problems to be resolved in taxing companies. If the income of some people who invest in companies is not to be over-taxed in a way that can also discourage overseas investors into the UK then the tax rate paid by UK companies (taking all comments already made into account) should always be above the standard rate of income tax that most people will pay on their wealth accumulations but below the higher rates that will be needed if vertical tax equity is to be established. The problem that this creates is immediately obvious: there is an incentive in this case for any person who pays higher rate tax who can arrange to reallocate their own income into a company to do so if they do not need immediate access to their wealth accumulation to meet living costs. People who do not need their income immediately are, of course, almost invariably amongst the wealthier members of any society; the simple existence of relatively low-taxed companies can increase income and wealth inequality unless action is taken to address the issue.

That problem can be solved by requiring that all the profits of a company with real, live, warm-blooded shareholders who have significant control of it, whether singly or as a group, should be apportioned to those members and be taxed as their own income in their own hands, with full credit for any tax paid anywhere in the world within the company being given for offset against any resulting UK tax bill (and with substantial penalties being payable for trying to circumvent this process). This process was familiar in UK company taxation from the 1960s to 1980s. Reinstating it, especially as company tax rates are falling around the world, is a precondition of tax justice.

Unfortunately that solution is impossible to apply in the case of larger companies where no such shareholders can be identified. In that case an excess profits tax should be charged when cash is retained in a company beyond the level that the logic of the existing group business requires. This, I accept, will not be an easy process but reflects the fact that there is no economic logic, barring tax saving, for companies to withhold profits from their members if they have no apparent use for them. Efficient markets do in fact require this distribution so that investors and not unknown managers can make the best choice of where their funds should be put to best use. Using this logic, business expansion has then to be subject to explicit shareholder approval, either for retaining funds or for raising new funding, as should always be true in any proper capital market. This excess profits tax is simply a reinforcement of desirable best business practice.

Doing these things solves many of the problems companies pose: but what about tax havens? This has been a perennial issue on which the tax justice movement has worked for more than a decade and I am not suggesting that the problem has gone away yet, but there has been progress. Multinational corporations are now to be required to submit country-by-country reporting accounts to HM Revenue & Customs that will show if they make use of such places: the chance of getting away with doing so reduces as a result. Similarly, as a result of civil society campaigning, the point has been reached where, very soon, tax havens will, in the vast majority of cases, be providing information on those people from the UK (and other similar countries) who maintain accounts in their jurisdictions. The simple fact is, the secrecy within them is being shattered. The chance to find a tax base has been created.

Bizarrely, some of the procedures that will now be required of tax havens are not as yet required within the UK economy. So, for example, whilst we will be expecting tax haven banks to provide information on the companies that are owned by UK-resident people to HM Revenue & Customs, we do not expect UK high-street banks to do the same thing, and this is absurd. They have these data: the time has come when it must be made available to our tax authority so that companies in the UK, which have for too long been, in effect, a cheap licensed form of identity theft when it comes to tax abuse – as a result of the exceptionally lax regulatory regime that the UK operates – are brought under control. The reality is that if we are willing to demand changes from tax havens so that they are transparent we must do the same within our own domestic economy to ensure that our tax authority has the best chance of catching tax cheats.

That, however, would be a complete waste of time if piles of information were sent to HM Revenue & Customs and they had no staff to use the data. There is widespread opinion, whether from the public, taxpayers, tax advisers or business, that HMRC is already under-staffed and has not got the resources to undertake the tasks expected of it. The recommendations I have already made will only add to the workload of HMRC. In particular, there is no point having better tax legislation and data to tackle tax avoidance if specialists are not available to use it, and likewise there is no point having additional information to tackle tax evasion unless staff resources, with relevant systems backup, are provided to make sure that the data can be used to trace those who are not paying their taxes. When HMRC has seen its staff numbers fall from more than 90,000 in 2005 to well below 60,000 in 2015, with the downward trend expected to continue,[5] those resources do not exist.

There are other issues to address as well. In particular, the wholesale withdrawal of HMRC from many communities in the UK represents a significant failure of the democratic process because taxpayers are now isolated from the body that asks them to pay tax when in practice HMRC should be seen to be operating in the communities that it serves, and that it expects to comply with its requirements.

For these reasons a radical review of the staffing of HMRC is now essential. It is very likely that as a result HMRC would be asked to reopen many of its offices in towns and cities up and down the UK, including those that provide the opportunity for taxpayers to have face-to-face meetings with tax officials to make sure that their affairs are properly managed. It is also the opinion of many tax professionals that HMRC should be provided with a substantial increase in the number of staff it has available to it to tackle tax avoidance, beat tax evasion, provide the level of service that UK taxpayers reasonably expect, recover tax debts and close the UK tax gap.

Estimates of the yield from employing those additional staff at HMRC vary but ARC, the union for its top-level staff, estimated[6] that at least £25 could be recovered for every additional £1 spent on one of their members in 2013. The yield might be lower overall if spending were to be on staff on other grades, as is also essential,[7] but no one seriously doubts that it would still be substantial.

This would, however, require a considerable change in the management culture in the upper echelons of HM Revenue & Customs. For archaic constitutional reasons, some of which were explored in Chapter 1, the UK is in the absurd position of having a tax authority that has no minister directly responsible for it and that has no Select Committee in Parliament to which it is directly accountable. The consequence, as has become all too apparent in recent years, is that the Board of HMRC has been unaccountable for its actions, and has been reluctant to explain itself to Parliament, or anyone else.

This lack of accountability has been compounded by the requirement that HMRC adopt a corporate-style structure since the time of its creation in 2005. This has encouraged the appointment of directors with little or no knowledge of tax, and the appointment of non-executive directors to its Board all of whom[8] are drawn from the large-business community even though there are only 700 such companies in the UK and 31 million taxpayers in all.

This corporate structure has very clearly failed. HMRC has failed to act in the public interest, as many hearings before the Public Accounts Committee have shown,[9] and has, too often, appeared to enter into cosy relationships with large companies[10] and high net worth individuals[11] that have resulted in them either enjoying what seem generous tax settlements or not being brought to account for the tax crimes that they may have committed. If there is to be confidence in the tax system in the United Kingdom then it is essential that this cosy relationship is ended between big business, its directors and tax advisers, and HMRC. It is also vital that HMRC is subject to proper scrutiny by Parliament in future.

Three steps are needed to achieve this goal. First, the Board of HMRC should be reconstituted so that it is representative of a broad range of taxpayers including large business, small business, employees, pensioners, civil society, charities, trade unions, the investment community and, of course, HMRC's staff. Only then can it really be considered suitable to direct the work of the department in the interests of the community as a whole.

Second, managing the government's revenue is too important a task for there to be no minister responsible for this activity in future. It is no longer acceptable that a junior Treasury minister be nominated to answer questions on the issue when they have no direct line of responsibility for HMRC. In that case HMRC must now become the responsibility of a full government department in its own right, independent of the Treasury. The resulting Department for Taxation should have a Cabinet minister responsible for answering for its actions. The minister in question must not be a member of the Treasury team, but must instead be accountable independently of that department for the success or failure of HMRC in achieving its forecasts and objectives.

Third, to ensure that HMRC is fully accountable to Parliament in future, there must be a Tax Select Committee of the House of Commons whose sole task should be to monitor tax policy and HMRC's success in collecting the tax revenues that are due in the UK, including an ongoing assessment of the UK tax gap. To achieve that goal the committee in question must overcome one of the anachronisms of the UK parliamentary system, which is that House of Commons Select Committees have almost no resources made available to them to research the work of the department whose activities they are meant to monitor.

If HMRC is to be held to account in future, both by a minister and by Parliament, then it is vital that an independent body, accountable to the minister, but jointly answerable to the Tax Select Committee of the House of Commons, should be created. The obvious name for such a body would be the Office for Tax Responsibility.

This Office for Tax Responsibility would have three main tasks. The first would be to monitor the likely effectiveness of proposed tax changes in more technical depth than the Office for Budget Responsibility does at present. The second would be to monitor the effectiveness of a tax law after implementation, to determine whether its objectives have been achieved and to make recommendations for further change if necessary. The third would be to independently appraise the tax gap and to monitor HMRC's effectiveness in allocating resources to close it, in ways that the National Audit Office never does at present. By undertaking these tasks this Office could finally make the UK tax system accountable, and not before time.

These changes are not enough in themselves to bring about all the reforms needed to deliver a fully working tax system. What I have outlined are the changes that are the prerequisite of that system working, without which the management of our economy will be harder, the achievement of any government's social and economic policies will be hindered, and the chances that tax will deliver all the benefits that it can provide for society will be impaired. To put it another way, we would not see the Joy of Tax in reality. So, reform is needed. But is that really possible? As I argue in my last chapter, I think it is.

9

As the Chancellor might put it

The preceding chapters have described an ideal tax system, and that, of course, is what everyone should aspire to. But, as the saying goes, if you really wanted an ideal tax system no one would choose to start from where we are now, despite which there is no alternative but to do just that. It follows that a massive programme of change in our tax system is needed.

Such a programme of change, as everything in this book might predict, would have to be big, and bold. It would require a courageous Chancellor, made in the mould I described in a previous book,[1] to deliver it. I don't know who that might be. All I can do is offer them, in this the final chapter of this book, the budget speech that they would need to make so that we might all share in the Joy of Tax. I just hope that whoever the Chancellor who takes up that challenge might be they will forgive me for ghost writing on their behalf. There is good reason for doing so: what I want to demonstrate is that what I have written so far is not abstract theory, but is the stuff of which politics is really made. So this is what I'd have that Chancellor say:

In the recent election the people of this country sent this House a clear and unambiguous message. They said that our tax system is a mess. They made clear that our benefits system is unfair. And they were unambiguous in demanding change to the way in which our economy works if it is to deliver the prosperity everyone in this country has a right to enjoy.

This budget is my response to those messages. It opens a new era in taxation in this country. For too long tax has been the subject of wrong-headed thinking, bad economics and poor design. From now on that will not be the case. This budget brings tax into the twenty-first century.

The Treasury will be publishing a full explanation of the economic foundations for this new tax system this afternoon, but let me tell the House what the principles are that underpin the changes in economic management that this government will begin to deliver today, and that will impact on the lives of every person in this country.

I must start with a little history. In 2014 the Bank of England had to admit that decades, and maybe centuries, of supposed understanding of how the banking system worked was plain straightforwardly wrong. They did in April that year recognize the essential truth that it is banks that create the money in our economy and that they do this by lending. What they realized was that money – every single penny of it – is created out of thin air by the simple process of debiting a loan account and crediting a current account whenever a loan is made by a bank.

This realization was in itself revolutionary. It says that if banks have such power then they very definitely need special attention from regulators, and tax authorities.

But more importantly, what it said is that there need never be a shortage of money in any economy. All the money we ever need to make things happen can be created out of thin air at the time it is required to make our economy work.

And it says governments can partake in this process as well, because we own the most important bank of all in the UK – the Bank of England.

In an instant the pretence that investment is only possible when there are sufficient savings in the economy to pay for it was shattered. We now know savings and investment are completely unrelated, except insofar as the Bank of England admitted that all bank deposits are made as a result of lending made, and not the other way round.

If you think about it that too is a revolutionary thought: what it says is that if banks fail through a lack of deposited funds to provide liquidity that's because of a lack of lending, and not a lack of saving.

Everything about banking was now admitted to be the opposite of everything that most people – including bankers, politicians and economists – had been saying to that date. And this was not because of a new development: what the Bank of England said was that people had always had this wrong.

And this has, let me assure you, a great deal to do with tax. That's because, I should remind you, government has always had the ability to create its own money, just as commercial banks do. Indeed, our right to create money pre-dated that of banks, and their right to create money only exists because we license them to do so.

But just saying that does, I hope, make three more economic truths very clear.

The first is that whilst commercial banks make money by lending, governments create cash by spending. That's the way the system works.

The second truth is this, that just as commercial banks limit the amount of money in the economy and so prevent it from spiralling out of control by requiring that their loans be repaid, so do governments do the same thing – but in their case they reclaim the money they have spent into the economy by claiming it back as taxation.

And thirdly, what this means is that government spending always comes before taxation, and is not dependent upon the amount of money that can be raised in tax.

In fact, it is always the case that, just as commercial banks can in theory always create the money that the economy needs if there is sufficient demand for borrowing, so too can the government always create the money it needs to fund anything it wants to do by spending the money that's required into existence.

But, and I can hear the House waiting for me to deliver a 'but', there is in all this a vital need to make sure that the economy does not run out of control. No one wants to live in an era of high inflation. No one wants the state to run out of control. No one wants boom and bust.

So there is a need for economic management in our national economy. That is what government is for. In fact, and let's be candid about this, there is no one else who can take on that role.

In that case this government does not believe it is our task to sit back and watch what the private sector might or might not do in this country and accept the consequences. Much as we believe in the private sector and a great deal of what it does, we do not think it can deliver what it is government's job to do.

Nor does this government think it is our job to only provide whatever services might be possible out of the taxes that the private sector might pay us after it has chosen to avoid and evade its responsibilities, as some amongst its membership have shown that they will.

Instead this government believes that it is our job to make sure that in partnership with the private sector – and I cannot stress that word partnership enough – we must create the conditions in which everyone, whether they be individuals, families, companies, young, old, able, disabled, men or women, and whatever their origin, belief or sexual orientation, can prosper in this country. We have a commitment to equality at the very heart of all that we do. That equality extends in our case to our belief in the role that the public and private sectors have to play in this country: we think their tasks are equal, and each is no more or less important than the other.

And that is why I am today presenting the radical proposals that I will describe before I sit down.

What we are saying is that, just as a private sector bank has to make a profit, but cannot do so without taking the risk of lending funds that may or may not be repaid in the future, so must we take the risk of spending in the expectation that tax will be paid in the future. But whereas the process of a bank reclaiming its loan is relatively simple because it is a business with no responsibility beyond those to its staff, customers, depositors and shareholders, we as a government have a much broader responsibility to everyone when we tax, which is how we reclaim our money.

As a result the tax that we reclaim from the economy has to achieve more than the simple task of recovering the money that we have spent, although economically that is what the process is all about. In taxing we think that it is our duty to make sure that we create the conditions for prosperity. And that we create the conditions for equality. And that we make sure we encourage the operation of free and effective markets whilst correcting for those issues, like pollution, that they can never control by themselves. And that we have to do all this accountably, because the overall decisions on what part of the economy should be taken up by government activity, and what proportion of our spending should be reclaimed by tax, will be decided at the end of the day by the people of this country at the ballot box, which is in our opinion the best place to decide what the right balance between the economic activity in the state and private sectors should be.

What all this means is that tax is not neutral. I welcome that fact. That means tax can, when required, raise more or less than government spending. What it need never be, and I cannot emphasize this strongly enough, is equal to spending simply for the sake of it.

If tax is less than government spending then that boosts the amount of activity in an economy. If that economy is not achieving to its potential and is not using, in particular, the skills and resources of all those who live within the state to best effect, then this has to be the most responsible act that a government can undertake. I stress the point: I believe we should tax less than we spend when otherwise the resources, talents and abilities of the people of this country would go to waste simply so that the books of the government can be balanced. To balance the books when that outcome would be the result would be a true national scandal.

And there is good reason for this. The simple fact is that government debt is something else that has been misunderstood by conventional economics. That's because government debt is not something we have to repay. That's the popular myth, but like the other popular myths on money and tax it is not true. The national debt is, in fact, just money. All money is debt. Nothing more. And nothing less. It's debt that makes money. And as we now know, repaying debt destroys money, literally. So let's be clear: government debt is just that part of the money supply that central government has created, just as commercial bank lending is the part of the money supply that the private sector has created.

Both matter and both have to be kept in check, but I stress the two are inextricably linked. Depending on the measure used, and I am not taking argument on that issue today, UK government debt may be 80 per cent of our national income at present,[2] up from 53 per cent in 2009. In contrast private debt was approximately 160 per cent of GDP in 2014,[3] which was, incidentally, a fall from 191 per cent in 2009. If you want the evidence that the growth in government money creation (more commonly called the national debt) is in large part substitution for private money destruction over that period, this is it. When the private sector was busy destroying our money stocks over this period, due to loan repayment, the government had no choice but to make good the shortfall if the economy was going to have the cash it needed.

But in that case what does that say about the argument for a balanced budget? It says that the balanced budget proponents are demanding that we should rely solely on banks to create money and that government should take no part in the process.

Think too about the argument for refusing to create new government debt (and so money) in that light. That's an argument that we should not only hand over ever-increasing responsibility for money creation to our banks but that we should accept whatever the outcome might be of that process – even if it were disastrous for our economy because there would simply not be enough money to keep it going.

Is that what we want? This government has a very clear response. It is a resounding no. As important as our banks are we know they have massive weaknesses. And we know that they do not, because they cannot, act in the national interest. So why on earth would anyone argue, as some do, that they should have sole responsibility for money creation? Not only is that politicians running away from their responsibility to act when it is necessary, this is a recipe for economic disaster. This government will not run away from its duties and will not deliberately create economic disaster. The economy is safe in our hands.

In which case, to avoid any doubt, please also understand that this means that, on occasion, it will be right that taxation is higher than government spending. That has to happen when the private sector has become too exuberant for our national good and is over-exciting the economy with new money resulting from record levels of commercial bank lending. I will welcome the day when the private sector does that because there are so many new products and services, as well as jobs, that it wants to create. But we have not seen it do that for a long time: at best it has only ever over-lent in recent times to fuel property speculation. I am asking the Governor of the Bank of England to put in place appropriate controls to address that issue, and when he has done this, I make this plea to business: 'I beg you: make us run a surplus because you're proving yourselves so able to deliver prosperity for this country.' But until the private sector does that I'll make things good for everyone in this country when the private sector will not.

So, when I run a government deficit it will be with pride, because I know that all I am doing is creating the cash, the jobs, the economic activity and the well-being that this country needs, when the private sector banks are not delivering because private business is not using the talents of the people of this country to best effect. That deficit spending will in that case be, I suggest, at the heart of responsible government. And it will never create debt that will burden future generations. It will just create money that the economy needs, in exactly the same way that private sector banks can do so.

So, saying all that, we will tax as much as is necessary and no more. And in raising that tax we will not just look to raise money, because that would be to presume that none of the other goals that this government has are of importance. Instead our tax policies will deliberately reflect our other policies, in all their diversity.

We will tax to increase equality, and in the process we will reduce inequality of income and wealth.

We will tax to encourage market activity, and to correct its failures.

We will tax to encourage full employment and opportunity for those who work.

We will tax to deliver sustainability because we and our children and their children require that.

We will tax to build sustainable growth.

We will tax openly and transparently.

We will tax for the common good, because that is what we believe tax can deliver.

So, what then do I propose to do to fulfil this vision? In essence what I am setting out today is a fundamental reform of taxation in this country because I believe that tax is fundamental to the prosperity of everyone, including everyone who trades, in the UK. This will be a new tax compact for the UK and the first of those reforms makes clear something about which it seems too many have been in denial in this country for too long. This reform makes clear that the money paid in tax in the UK is money that the government owns: it is not taxpayers' money.

In case there is doubt after what I have just said, let me spell this out: the government spends its own money. That is made up of money it can create, money it can borrow and money it collects in tax. But in each and every case what it spends is money belonging to the government. It is not the taxpayers'. The myth that somehow it is the taxpayers' money that the government uses has been very convenient for those who argue that they could make better use of the cash in question, an argument they then take as justification for avoidance or evasion of their obligation to pay. I have to tell all who think that: from today think again. Taxes that are owed from now on are due because the tax in question belongs to the government and not you, and I am here to remind everyone that we were given the right to collect that tax by the people of this country in free and democratic elections and you're cheating on your neighbours if you want to pretend otherwise. Your neighbours don't like cheats and nor do we. That's why we're changing the rules of tax.

Like many Chancellors before me I am not amused by the work of a vast army of highly paid lawyers, bankers and accountants who think it their job to undermine my right to tax, even though that right has been granted by the people of this country. Time and again my predecessors have tried to tackle this problem, but all have failed. Our tax law is as a result incredibly long, and deeply complex. The reason for that is that no one has, until today, had the courage to challenge the cause of this problem at its root. That root is that UK tax law is written so that nothing is taxable unless the law says it is.

This is what I am going to change. I now advise the House that we are going to introduce a new law. It will be called the Tax Base Act. And it will say that all income, profits, gains, gifts, wealth, land, sales and other such tax bases are in the scope to tax unless specifically exempted. The result is that, for the very first time, if a taxpayer argues that something they have done is not taxable it will be for them to prove that is the case: the onus will now be on them whereas in the past it has always been the government's duty to prove that tax was due. The same law will also say that nothing can be offset against a tax bill unless specifically allowed by law. Again, if there is doubt it will be for the taxpayer to prove their case. The whole balance of power in UK taxation will change for ever as a result, but the vast majority of us will not notice because we have always lived very comfortably within the law as it is. For tax cheats I am, however, creating the proverbial nightmare scenario, and I am sure that most people in this country will be delighted as a result.

To back this up I will ensure that in future all UK tax law will be purposive. That means every bit of new law will say why it is being introduced, what it is meant to achieve, and why that is necessary.

And to back all this up I will introduce a second Act. This will be called the Interpretation of Tax Law Act, and will make clear that, when dispute arises, all tax cases will be decided on whether or not the intention of the law has been complied with. HM Revenue & Customs will not be able to demand a payment by claiming that a law has a meaning no one in this House ever intended it should have. And a taxpayer will not be able to claim exemption from tax or a right to offset an expense unless they can show that this was intended.

At a stroke I will add to the certainty of tax law. It will be simpler. It will be shorter. It will be clearer. It will make its case in plain English so it can be understood. And it will be guided by principles that anyone will be capable of making sense of.

Of course this is a big change. It will require consultation. And we will go out of our way to hear the opinion of all who need to be consulted on this issue, and not just the views of the tax profession and big business who are usually the only people who can afford the time and effort to take part in these processes. To achieve this we will be awarding grants to make sure that those who think they need to be heard when we ask for opinion will have the chance to get their say, not just on this issue but on others of similar significance over time.

That open-mindedness to all who have interest in tax is something that I believe must extend throughout the tax system. For that reason I am also announcing a major change to the way in which HMRC is managed today. It is absurd that this department – one of the biggest in Whitehall – has no minister to whom it is responsible. Chancellors, and their teams, have answered for it over the years, but there is no minister for taxation. Nor is there a Department of Taxation. Instead we have our tax authority run by a Board. To whom that Board is responsible is not clear. And how Parliament gets to hold them to account is even more ambiguous: it has not even been possible to decide which committee can ask them questions. There may have been historical reasons for this – just as there are for the fact that HMRC is still named as if the personal property of our sovereign – but such anachronisms belong to another age and will not do in the twenty-first century.

So today I am announcing that we are creating a new Secretary of State for Taxation. My Right Honourable friend the Prime Minister will be announcing who will hold the appointment in due course. That minister will be supported by the usual range of ministerial colleagues and together they will be responsible for running the new Department of Taxation, whose job it will be to collect the taxes for which HMRC has been responsible since 2005.

Such a Department could not function without a proper statement of purpose. That I will clearly state. The new Department of Taxation will be tasked with collecting all those taxes rightly due from those who owe them under UK law wherever they might reside, whatever nationality they might have, and whatever legal status they might claim. In doing so it shall be expected to apply the law equitably and with due sensitivity to the taxpayer's position. It will be obliged to provide help to those who make reasonable request for support in paying their tax. It will be allowed to charge for doing so when it is reasonable that it might do so. And it will, of course, be held to account by an independent appeals and judicial system, with whose rulings it will be obliged to comply. Tax justice will be at the heart of UK taxation from now on.

To ensure that the new Secretary of State and ministerial colleagues are appropriately advised we will establish a new advisory board to replace that which previously oversaw HMRC, but we will not replicate that Board's membership, which was exclusively reserved for tax advisers and representatives of big business. This new Board will seek to recruit membership reflecting the interests of all taxpayers. The days when our tax authority appeared to be run by big business and the wealthy for the benefit of the best-off in society have to be consigned to history.

The new Department will have some very clear budget responsibilities placed upon it. It will be expected to estimate what the total sum owing in tax in any year might be and set out clearly how best it might manage its resources to collect that sum. When, as will inevitably happen on occasion, it falls short of that total sum it will be expected to explain why this tax gap has arisen and what it intends to do to remedy the deficit, if that is possible. This will include recommending new law and the repeal of old law that has outlived its purpose.

To make sure that these complex issues are fully understood by my new ministerial colleagues, and, as importantly, the Members of this House, we will create a new Office for Tax Responsibility. This will report jointly to the Secretary of State and a new Select Committee of this House. This Office will audit HMRC, the tax gap and the new Department's effectiveness in using resources. It will also vet and comment upon that Department's proposals for change in tax law. It will be entitled in its own right to suggest those laws that now need reform or repeal. And to make sure this House has the say that it deserves on this most vital of issues the new Select Committee will be allowed to ask this Office for Tax Responsibility to undertake reviews on its behalf.

The Chancellor will retain overall responsibility for establishing economic policy for the UK: tax is just a part of that process but it is an important one. The new minister and I will work very closely together.

In doing so I make clear that I will reverse another of my predecessors' policies in place over many years. We will treat the Department of Taxation as a revenue department and not as one that incurs expense. As such, it will be granted the resources it needs to undertake its job, so long as it can show that these resources will be used cost-effectively. The days when we have run a deficit because we have not allocated enough money to collecting the taxes due in this country are over.

Changing the administration of tax will not, however, be enough to fulfil our plans to collect the tax owing in this country. Some serious and systemic defects in the tax system will also need to be addressed. So, for example, every company and trust in the UK will be required to submit a tax return in future. And every bank in the UK shall be obliged to tell the new Department for Taxation who they have identified as the directors and owners of those companies. Those people will then be liable for all the tax owing by their companies if it is not paid and they cannot prove this was not through their own neglect. The process by which UK companies could be used to help anyone who wanted to evade tax from behind a veil of anonymity must be brought to an end.

For the same reason all companies will be required to put their full accounts, including expanded information on their tax due and paid, on public record in future. In the case of multinational corporations this will mean that they will have to file accounts including country-by-country reporting data.

And, because the accountancy profession has failed to deliver these reforms, we will no longer trust them to deliver the accounting standards to ensure tax is properly paid in this country in due course. They may, of course, continue to set International Financial Reporting Standards and UK Generally Accepted Accounting Principles but we are today setting up a Tax Reporting Standards Board to make sure that we get the accounting data we need to ensure that tax due is both paid and properly explained in the accounts of all who trade in the UK.

Let me move on to discuss just who we think those taxable in the UK might be. I can announce that from today we are abolishing the domicile rule that has allowed some people to claim a special and restricted basis for taxation in this country on the grounds of the accident of their situation at birth. That type of discrimin-ation has no place in the UK in the twenty-first century. A new temporary residence rule will, however, be available to those here for less than five complete tax years.

Deciding which companies are resident in the UK has always been a sensitive issue and international law has not kept pace with it. I therefore announce today that we will now consider all companies and trusts that own land and buildings in the UK or which employ people in the UK to be resident in the UK and that, without exception, all such companies will be required to file their accounts on public record in this country, making clear what part of their income and profit arises in the UK, and all will be required to file UK tax returns, irrespective of which other countries they might have tax obligations to. We will be proposing multilateral reform to our double tax treaties with all other countries impacted by this change, offering them reciprocal rights. We stress, we are only seeking to tax that part of their income that arises in the UK to UK tax, but the time when trading in the UK could be used as a mechanism to avoid tax that might otherwise be due in this country has to be brought to an end.

So too do many of the opportunities to shift profits out of the UK need to be brought to an end. Most of these arise when expenses are claimed for tax purposes that have been charged to a company trading in the UK from companies to which they are related that are located elsewhere. To tackle this issue I can confirm that we are also seeking multilateral change to our double tax treaties. This will ensure that tax may be deducted at source from payments of interest, dividends, royalties, management charges, insurance premiums and hedging expenses when paid from the UK to companies related to that making the payment located in a wide range of countries that we have identified as having insufficiently stringent tax regimes to ensure that those sums are appropriately taxed on receipt. We will willingly offer reciprocal rights to the countries affected. The curse of profit-shifting has to be brought to an end: the UK must have the right to tax profit arising in this country. For the time being the European Union is outside the scope of this change, but we will be raising this issue with our partners there.

To ensure that this right to tax is upheld I also announce that the UK's General Anti-Abuse Rule will be replaced with a General Anti-Avoidance Principle. This might sound semantic, but it is not: the abuse rule puts the onus of proof of abuse on our tax authority. The general anti-avoidance principle will require a taxpayer to show that each step in a transaction has not been included for tax reasons and does instead have a substantial alternative purpose or it will be ignored when tax is due. The age of tax avoidance has to be brought to an end. This is an important step in achieving that goal.

Let me finally turn then to the taxes we will charge in this country and state the principles on which we will charge them. That's necessary because many of our taxes make little or no sense now, having been designed in other eras for economic circumstances long forgotten. Too often they are discriminatory: tax on those working for a living has long been much higher in this country than that due on similar sums enjoyed by people living off investment income, gains or speculation. That makes no sense at all. If we are to have a fair and progressive tax system in the UK then a pound that a person receives should not be taxed more or less favourably dependent upon the place from which it comes or the way in which it is recorded unless there is very sound public benefit for that difference.

In that case some UK taxes need abolition now. One of those is capital gains tax. Capital gains will in future be taxed as income. A small annual allowance of tax-free gains will be permitted in future, purely to save the cost of having to report all gains, however small they might be, for tax purposes, but the idea that the conversion of income into gains should reduce tax rates will come to an end.

This change will, I stress, apply to the sale of private businesses: as the likes of Warren Buffett have pointed out, no true entrepreneur was ever put off their goal by the fact that they might have to pay fair tax at some point on the money they made.

Anti-avoidance measures to prevent the shifting of gains in marriages and civil partnerships and the shifting of gains outside the UK on the sale of UK assets will be introduced, with those responsible for aiding and abetting the latter being made liable for all the tax owing on any arrangement they have helped create.

Back in 1965 when capital gains tax was created it made sense to exempt a person's home from charge to this tax. This country was not then the home-owning nation the government of the day wished it to be, and there was a need to build new houses. We wanted to provide that opportunity and an incentive to take it. Property wealth was surprisingly limited. There was a desire to spread it more widely. Times have changed. This country has become one where property represents a significant part of private wealth, but precisely because of the tax relief provided in 1965 that wealth is now hugely concentrated in an ageing minority who can still afford to own their own home. Many of the young now have no chance of owning a house precisely because, after fifty years of tax-free gains having accumulated in the property market, house prices have moved way beyond their reach. What was once a good idea is now a bad idea that is creating social and inter-generational stress in the UK. As a result gains arising from today on UK housing will be taxable. But, because I know that people need to move for many reasons during their lives, we will only collect the tax due when a person dies or when they do not reinvest the proceeds of the sale of their house in another home. No one will be denied the chance to live in a house to the value they have been accustomed to owning because of this tax charge.

Capital gains will also apply to the sale of all agricultural land and businesses in future, and upon the gift of all assets whether during life or on death. In the case of owner-managed businesses and family-run farms we recognize that continuity of management is important, and that businesses should not be denuded of capital as a result of tax owing. Consequently we will make special arrangements in these cases to accept part-ownership of the assets sold or gifted in lieu of taxes, but we do make clear that such ownership will be actively managed to ensure that the state receives its share of future profits, and special rights shall be attached to any shares accepted as part of such an arrangement to ensure that these rights can be enforced.

With these changes to capital gains tax there will be little reason for inheritance tax in the future and as a result I confirm that this tax, which has been the cause of much vexation, will be abolished.

In place of this tax I am instead proposing a wealth tax. This is now possible for the first time because of the information-sharing agreements that we now have with so many of the world's tax havens. We will pursue such deals with those that have still not signed them. In the meantime any professional adviser who in any way assists a person to avoid tax by exploiting the remaining states who have not cooperated with us will under new arrangements become personally liable for all tax not paid as a consequence, without limit.

The wealth tax will not be charged on main residences, family farms and private businesses that will now be subject to capital gains tax in life, whether gifted or sold, and on death. Nor will it be charged on pension wealth. This charge will then be on let-property portfolios, financial investment portfolios, personal property and other assets of similar type primarily used to generate unearned income, unless they are otherwise exempted by law using the new principles for writing tax law that I have already outlined. The charge will be introduced on all such portfolios worth more than £1 million at the rate of 1 per cent per annum, although the rate will increase with the scale of declared wealth. All wealth will be subject to self-declaration. Any assets not declared will become the property of the state. Any asset under-valued will be subject to sale to the state at the under-declared price if the Department of Taxation decides to exercise that option. Wealth will be calculated on a worldwide basis.

I have three further measures relating to land to announce before moving on. The first relates to council tax. This is a tax produced in a hurry by a government in a panic that nobody has dared revise since the day that it was introduced in 1992 and which is unfit for purpose today, and as unfair now as on the day it was created. It makes no sense at all that this tax, which is charged on the occupiers and not the owners of land, and which encourages second-property ownership and properties being left vacant, whilst the fact that charges are capped at what are now ludicrously low valuations renders it regressive, should continue in existence. I can therefore confirm that arrangements are to be made to introduce a land value tax in England and that devolved governments will be encouraged to consider similar taxes in the parts of the country for which they are responsible. Such a change will take time, and care will be needed with the design of this tax. This means that its introduction will be delayed for at least three years, but I can set out its design principles now. All land will, without exception, be liable to this tax, although exemptions for some land and uses will be made, using our new tax design principles. Any land where the beneficial owner (including the owners of offshore companies) cannot be identified will be held by the Crown in trust until ownership can be established. If that has not happened within ten years the state will become the legal owner of the land in question. The tax will be charged on the rental value of the undeveloped land: this is a tax on land and not on buildings. The tax will be progressive: the higher the value of the land the higher the rate will be. Land will not be aggregated for assessment: the wealth tax addresses that issue, in our opinion. The rates of tax will be deliberately set to ensure that many living in lower-banded council tax property will pay less in future and all tenants will, by definition, be exempted from this tax. Arrangements will be made to prevent landlords passing on their liabilities to their tenants.

The next change with regard to land relates to stamp duty. Because all housing will now be subject to capital gains tax, keeping the stamp duty charge on the purchase and sale of private houses makes no sense at all, so it will be abolished. In combination these two changes considerably reduce the cost of moving house in the UK if a person needs to relocate for the purposes of their employment, and will as a result help people find work to suit their needs and to relocate when family or other needs demand it.

I have two final changes to make with regard to housing. The first tackles the illogical fact that interest relief on mortgage borrowings has been provided to landlords for the last twenty-five years when it has been denied to owner-occupiers. This makes no sense at all. It divides the market, has fuelled house price increases by subsidizing the cost of buy-to-let arrangements and has driven a massive increase in housing benefit costs as a result. Previous governments have restricted this relief to basic rate tax, but I now intend to abolish it for everyone bar not-for-profit landlords. I am aware, of course, that this will cause stress to some landlords. For those affected we will offer a guarantee: we will buy properties from distressed landlords where there are tenants in place for the value of the mortgage outstanding as at today's date or 80 per cent of market value, whichever is the higher. No one need face financial crisis as a result of this change.

The move will, however, create a potential shortage of new housing for let. This will be addressed by the launch of a house-building programme to be funded by infrastructure quantitative easing. The debt that not-for-profit social landlords (including local authorities and housing associations) issue to fund their programmes will be made available for sale on financial markets in future, but with a guarantee that so long as the properties meet minimum requirements, including high environmental standards, a new Investment Bank to be established today will fund those loans using new money especially created for the purpose by the Bank of England. Every government has the power to create money for social purposes. We will use it when it provides a proper and better alternative than taxation provides.

Let me turn then to other taxes. I have made clear our policies. We are not seeking to balance our budget, although the quantitative easing programme I have just announced will, by taking a burden off taxation, make it more likely that we will achieve that goal. I stress: our tax policy will always be designed to ensure that we can deliver high-quality jobs in every constituency in the UK while also ensuring that those with needs that the government can help with have access to the resources they require, whatever they might be. This is our priority: people working matters more than balancing a budget.

This, though, means I have major changes to make in the structure of the UK's tax system. First let me deal with income tax, which many think to be at the heart of that system. Income tax is one of our few progressive taxes at present, and as such plays a vital role in delivering the essential redistribution of income in this country that is a foundation of our common wealth. I wish to reinforce that process. Firstly, the anomaly where some on higher income in the UK are denied a personal allowance for the purposes of this tax must go. Everyone will now enjoy that allowance.

Equally, it is absurd that some get more value from this allowance than others because they are higher rate taxpayers. That denies the fact that we should all be treated as equals by the tax system: this allowance will now only be available at the basic rate of tax.

That precedent is one I want to build on: in future no allowance or relief, excepting those given as a deduction from trading income, will be provided at anything but the basic rate of tax. This will provide an enormous simplification to our current tax regime as well as delivering social justice.

On the subject of such allowances and reliefs, now that we know, as the Bank of England has admitted, that savings are not the precondition of investment in the UK economy, but that credit is, the economic justification for many of the savings arrangements that receive favourable treatment in the UK tax system has disappeared. Moreover, since, by definition, most of those using these schemes can already afford to save, the tax relief provided tends simply to increase wealth inequality in the UK. That's the exact opposite of the policy we intend to pursue. As such all such reliefs, including those for pension saving, will be phased out over the next five years. I have been persuaded to retain the ISA scheme that can be used by many as an alternative mechanism for saving for retirement, although I would stress my own belief that much of the money in ISAs would be saved anyway, meaning that the tax relief provided is simply a state subsidy to no good effect for those not in need of it. I will establish several parallel studies on this issue in the near future to determine whether or not my hypothesis is correct, to ensure that money is not being wasted unnecessarily in keeping this scheme.

Investment income has, in any case, been incredibly favourably treated in the last thirty years in the UK because unlike earnings from work it has not been subject to national insurance. I can see no economic justification for this, or the half-hearted attempt to address this issue that the dividend tax introduced by a predecessor represented. I announce the abolition of that tax today. I also announce that there will now be, so long as we have a national insurance charge in this country, an investment income surcharge on all types of unearned income, including interest, dividends, rents, trust distributions and taxable proceeds from insurance policies. This will be set at a rate broadly equivalent to 60 per cent of the combined employee's and employer's national insurance contribution. The first £3,000 of investment income will be exempt from the charge for those below retirement age. That will increase to an exemption equivalent to median annual income for pensioners.

The relationship between the tax and national insurance systems has always been difficult, and national insurance is now a tax without economic justification. It no longer funds pensions or the NHS, and the mechanisms for its payment reflect a world of work long gone. It's especially worrying that it discourages employment when high-quality work for all has to be our national goal. I want therefore to announce that it is my plan to abolish national insurance charges. This goal will not, however, be achieved overnight. This change is too big for that to be the case and we cannot do without a means to collect the revenue national insurance currently contributes.

I have considered merging income tax and national insurance, but that will not do. Firstly, national insurance is a regressive tax and any merger would to some degree reproduce that in income tax. Secondly, the resulting rates would be unattractively high.

I am instead introducing a new tax. This is a

progressive charge on financial flows through bank accounts and related payment systems. The charge will apply to individuals and businesses. Initially the rate charged will be flat above a fixed sum flowing through all an individual's linked accounts – the link ensuring that account transfers can go on unimpeded. The fixed sum will be designed to ensure that for many on lower incomes this charge will not apply. Over time the rate will become progressive: the goal will be to entirely replace the regressive national insurance charge that at present discourages employment with a new progressive charge that will discourage excessive consumption in a way that no tax in the UK does at present. We know that this is necessary: we cannot afford the excess consumption that is fuelling global warming. This is a tax whose time has come. That is why I am going to call it a Carbon Usage Tax, or CUT for short. Measures to beat avoidance of this tax, including avoidance by the transfer of banking arrangements outside the UK, will be put in place.

Anti-avoidance arrangements are also needed when it comes to company taxation. Another anomaly of UK taxation has been that anyone can transfer their income from their own name into that of a company they own and reduce their tax rate as a result. This makes no sense: a pound under a person's control is always worth the same amount to them, whether in a company or not, and that pound should be subject to the same tax wherever it is recorded. Our economy is being distorted by this situation, and almost certainly to our disadvantage.

When corporation tax was first introduced so too was the concept of the close company. This was any company controlled by five or fewer people – with all close relatives counting as one person. I intend to revive the idea: all close companies will from now on have their income apportioned to their members, who will have to pay tax on their share whether or not they are paid it. I am aware this could create injustice: as a result all companies that distribute less than 50 per cent of their taxable income to their shareholders will instead see their corporation tax rate double in future and the shareholders will be discharged from their responsibility in that case. To make sure that such companies are not prevented from investing I will ensure that all companies impacted have 100 per cent allowances on their capital spending and that it is only taxable income that they need distribute, not their accounting profits. Nothing in this arrangement will harm the entrepreneurial economy.

For larger companies there are obvious problems in applying this rule. Their tax needs to be dealt with in a different fashion entirely, and in due course I intend that large and small company tax regimes should be separate for that reason. For now I make clear that the first steps in addressing this problem will be an increase in the corporation tax rate for such companies. These companies impose a cost on society because they can reduce the effectiveness of taxation systems. They also impose a cost because of the risks limited liability creates. And their members secure a benefit from both situations: this benefit needs to be paid for. Consequently a 5 per cent excess tax will be due by these companies on all their profits chargeable in the UK. Coupled with the measures already noted to secure the UK tax base, I expect this to increase significantly their contribution to the UK economy.

That is important: we have people in need in the UK and I intend to help them. For too long our UK social security system has been characterized as being inhabited by those who are work shy or scroungers. I know that is simply not true. Of course there are a few to whom such terms might apply, but it's insulting to the vast majority on low income and who need support in this country to even suggest that such terms have general application. Instead of permitting such allegations by seeking to separate the benefits system from the majority in society I wish to make clear that the benefits and tax systems should instead be seen as a continuum by integrating them. The goal is to guarantee a minimum income to everyone in the UK, whoever they are, and whatever age they are, so long as they have a minimum residence qualification. Such a move will have enormous advantages: in particular the penal tax rates suffered by those moving from benefits into work will largely disappear whilst the stigma of old age and pensions will eventually be replaced by a national income all will share.

I will say now that this will, of course, increase income tax rates: I accept that as the price for social justice for each and every person in this country. But every single person will also be in receipt in due course of a minimum guaranteed income that will protect everyone from the curse of poverty. I can think of nothing more important that a government can do for the young, the old, the vulnerable, the unfortunate, the disabled and those whom the market has failed than this. That is why we will set out to achieve this goal.

I recognize I cannot do it overnight, but we will do three things today. First we will restore universal child credits. Second we will eliminate many of the penal elements that have crept into the benefits system such as the much hated bedroom tax that has victimized so many, and third I will ensure that everyone of adult age will now enjoy the value of the personal allowance that I have also granted to those on highest pay today. So, if a person in receipt of benefits will from today have insufficient taxable income to receive the cash value of the personal allowance given to all with income at the basic rate in tax then their income will be topped up by this amount, in cash. The income tax system in this country is not just for those in work: it is for everyone, and so too is the benefits system. We have begun today the march to make them one system that ensures everyone in this country can live in dignity.

Finally, let me turn to those taxes that impact on spending. I have already mentioned a new tax on bank deposits. It would be inappropriate to create such a tax without recognizing the special status of the financial services industry when it comes to such a tax. The sums contracted in this sector are out of all proportion to those in the rest of the economy, or world come to that. It has long been suggested that this country needs a financial transactions tax. Today it gets one, with differential rates for trading in shares and other securities, foreign exchange, derivatives and other futures, to allow flexibility in the response that this tax can provide to each of these markets. I am also commissioning research on how such rates may be varied in times of high-volume trading to slow down markets when they are tending to panic. This tax is as much about preventing the excesses that these markets cause as it is about revenues raised, although I expect the sums in question to be significant. As a state with its own currency we will put in place necessary anti-avoidance measures to ensure that this tax will be hard to avoid or evade.

Our biggest tax on consumption is VAT. This is a tax that has raised significant sums and which many economists have said should be reformed to remove the exemptions and allowances within it which they say create economic inefficiencies. I have to disagree. If economic efficiency means lots of money irrespective of ability to pay and simplicity means taxing come what may then I might agree with the economists who say this, but I do not, of course, think those terms mean anything like that. So we will, of course, retain VAT but I intend to reduce the rate to the lowest levels allowed by the European Union and will compensate by increasing the bank transactions tax on consumption. VAT has contributed to the quite absurd situation where the UK has what looks like a flat tax system overall, except at the bottom end where it is obviously regressive. I intend to change that and this is a first step in this direction.

There are specific measures I will take to increase specific expenditure taxes but at this moment, given the scale of other tax reforms already announced, these must be relatively minor and can only be justified by policy need. One such need is to reform our basis of air transport taxation. This is a flat tax and makes a relatively high charge on families going on their annual holiday and a low one in proportion to income on those who travel frequently. So I am pleased to announce a new progressive air usage tax. Anyone flying once a year will now pay no airport taxes; those who travel frequently will pay progressive rates of tax based on their passport data which will be collected at the time of booking for that purpose.

I will also tackle one other pressing issue and that is

tax on renewable energy. The climate change levy is charged on this at present. That is absurd: the levy will be removed immediately.

I am open to suggestions on other such changes. Please send them my way. Our tax system will from now on be open, accountable and up for discussion, just as all today's announcements will be subject to appropriate consultation. In saying that I do, however, return to my opening themes.

This is a budget that sets out to change our understanding of tax and its role in our society for good. It is a budget that says that a government has a duty to manage the economy of the nation it has been elected to govern, and it confirms that this government will do that. It's a budget that rejects the false logic of balancing the books, and says that there are more ways than just taxing to do that in any case: our use of quantitative easing to fund social housing announced today is evidence of that. In due course we expect to use the same mechanism for other purposes.

But most of all this is a budget about fairness. It will redistribute income and wealth, but in ways that are appropriate. It will encourage work, but provide for those who cannot work or for whom work is not paying appropriately in ways that respect them as the fully valued members of society that they are. It creates a level playing field between business and the rest of the community, and between the UK and its partners. And by taking taxes off work and putting them onto excess consumption this is a budget about achieving the potential of all people in this country, and not about delivering the chance for a few to spend a lot.

As such this budget is about our common future and building it together. That's what I call the Joy of Tax.

I commend the Joy of Tax to the House.

Notes and sources

Chapter 1: Tax and society

1 http://www.bbc.co.uk/schools/gcsebitesize/science/
   21c_pre_2011/evolution/theoryevolutionrev1.shtml
   accessed 12 August 2014
2 http://www.nhm.ac.uk/nature-online/life/human-origins/
   modern-human-evolution/when/index.html
3 http://www.upenn.edu/almanac/v48/n28/AncientTaxes.
   html
4 http://www.taxresearch.org.uk/Blog/2009/11/18/
   a-theology-of-taxation/ and links
5 e.g. Exodus 30:15 and Nehemiah 10:33
6 Genesis 41:34
7 Amos 5:11 and 7:1
8 1 Kings 4:7
9 Leviticus 27:30–32
10 2 Kings 15:20
11 2 Kings 23:35
12 http://www.upenn.edu/almanac/v48/n28/AncientTaxes.
   html

13 Based on Clifford Ando, 'The Administration of the Provinces', in *A Companion to the Roman Empire* (Blackwell, 2010) as quoted on Wikipedia http://en.wikipedia.org/wiki/Roman_Empire#Taxation accessed 13 August 2014

14 http://www.sheshen-eceni.co.uk/boudica_info.html accessed 13 August 2014

15 Matthew 17:27

16 Romans 13:7

17 http://en.wikipedia.org/wiki/Charter_of_Liberties

18 http://magnacarta.cmp.uea.ac.uk/read/magna_carta_1215/Clause_12

19 http://magnacarta.cmp.uea.ac.uk/read/magna_carta_1215/Clause_14

20 http://www.nationalarchives.gov.uk/pathways/citizenship/citizen_subject/origins.htm

21 http://www.archives.gov/exhibits/charters/declaration_transcript.html

22 http://www.scotland.gov.uk/Resource/0042/00422987.pdf

23 http://www.hmrc.gov.uk/manuals/cgmanual/cg22100.htm

24 For more ideas on this theme refer to *Taxation and State-building in Developing Countries* by Deborah Brautigam, Odd-Helgre Fjeldstad and Mick Moore, Cambridge University Press, 2008

Chapter 2: What is tax?

1 http://www.telegraph.co.uk/finance/personalfinance/9845624/Top-14-per-cent-of-taxpayers-pay-60-per-cent-of-all-tax.html

2 http://budgetresponsibility.org.uk/economic-fiscal-out-

look-march-2014

3 http://www.oxforddictionaries.com/definition/english/tax

4 http://www.bbc.co.uk/news/magazine-24135021

5 http://www.washingtonpost.com/blogs/answer-sheet/wp/2013/10/01/589-days-with-no-elected-government-what-happened-in-belgium

6 An idea I have borrowed from John F. Kennedy, quoted at http://www.jfklibrary.org/Research/Research-Aids/Ready-Reference/JFK-Quotations/Profiles-in-Courage-quotations.aspx based on page 265 of his posthumous book *Profiles in Courage*

7 http://news.bbc.co.uk/onthisday/hi/dates/stories/march/31/newsid_2530000/2530763.stm

8 http://economia.icaew.com/news/november-2012/tax-avoidance-schemes-no-go-area-for-firms

9 http://en.wikipedia.org/wiki/List_of_countries_by_GDP_(nominal)_per_capita

10 http://en.wikipedia.org/wiki/List_of_countries_by_tax_revenue_as_percentage_of_GDP

11 https://www.gov.uk/government/policies/spending-tax-payers-money-responsibly

Chapter 3: Why we tax

1 http://www.bankofengland.co.uk/monetarypolicy/Pages/qe/default.aspx accessed 20 August 2014

2 All data compiled by the author from HM Treasury budget reports over the years in question

3 http://www.bankofengland.co.uk/about/pages/default.aspx. The Bank of England was nationalized after the Second World War. There are conspiracy theorists who claim this never really happened and that it remains under private control. Some people also believe there are fairies

at the bottom of their garden.

4 Values go up and down depending on the age of the debt, its nominal interest rate and the current market rate for debt of that age.

5 Money is, quite literally, created out of thin air by the making of loans. I have explained the process on my blog http://www.taxresearch.org.uk/Blog/2011/06/17/all-money-is-a-confidence-trick-2/. I, with others, campaigned to have this fact officially recognized by the Bank of England and they finally did so in their first Quarterly Bulletin for 2014 in which they also admitted that quantitative easing – the process by which £375 billion of government debt was reacquired by the Bank of England – was effectively a money-printing exercise. http://www.bankofengland.co.uk/publications/documents/quarterly bulletin/2014/qb14q1prereleasemoneycreation.pdf

6 http://www.bankofengland.co.uk/publications/Pages/quarterlybulletin/2014/qb14q1.aspx accessed 21 August 2015

7 In April 2014 the Bank of England said:

In the modern economy, most money takes the form of bank deposits. But how those bank deposits are created is often misunderstood: the principal way is through commercial banks making loans. Whenever a bank makes a loan, it simultaneously creates a matching deposit in the borrower's bank account, thereby creating new money.

The reality of how money is created today differs from the description found in some economics textbooks:

- Rather than banks receiving deposits when

households save and then lending them out, bank lending creates deposits.

- In normal times, the central bank does not fix the amount of money in circulation, nor is central bank money 'multiplied up' into more loans and deposits.

Although commercial banks create money through lending, they cannot do so freely without limit. Banks are limited in how much they can lend if they are to remain profitable in a competitive banking system. Prudential regulation also acts as a constraint on banks' activities in order to maintain the resilience of the financial system. And the households and companies who receive the money created by new lending may take actions that affect the stock of money – they could quickly 'destroy' money by using it to repay their existing debt, for instance.

http://www.bankofengland.co.uk/publications/Documents/quarterlybulletin/2014/qb14q102.pdf

8 John K. Galbraith, in *Money: Whence it came, where it went*, Houghton Mifflin, 1975, p. 29

9 It can be argued that there is a cost in paying interest at bank rate (currently 0.5%) on the new reserves created at the Bank of England as a result of the funds injected into the economy by the quantitative easing process, but as (Lord) Adair Turner has pointed out, the payment of this interest is optional and a choice by the Bank of England. http://www.socialeurope.eu/2014/03/monetization

10 http://budgetresponsibility.org.uk/pubs/March_2014_EFO_Charts_and_Tables.xls table T1.4 accessed 21 August 2014

11 Some of the author's work on the issue of shadow economies worldwide is available at http://www.tackletaxhavens.com/Cost_of_Tax_Abuse_TJN%20Research_23rd_Nov_2011.pdf

12 Abstract of Lincoln's Monetary Policy; Library of Congress No. 23, 76th Congress, 1st session, page 91; quoted at http://cpe.us.com/?article=famous-monetary-quotes. The rest is worth reading as well.

13 Sample measures of inequality – called the Gini coefficient – for a range of countries both before and after tax are available at http://en.wikipedia.org/wiki/List_of_countries_by_income_equality accessed 21 August 2014

Chapter 4: Dealing with the naysayers

1 http://www.iea.org.uk/sites/default/files/publications/files/ upldbook350pdf.pdf

2 http://www.adamsmith.org/blog/liberty-justice/democracys-not-all-its-cracked-up-to-be-you-know

3 http://www.adamsmith.org/blog/politics-government/democracy-must-restrain-the-mob-against-the-minority

4 http://www.2020tax.org

5 http://www.theguardian.com/business/2013/jan/08/climate-change-debt-inequality-threat-financial-stability

6 http://www.ons.gov.uk/ons/dcp171778_317365.pdf

7 http://www.ifs.org.uk/bns/bn43.pdf page 4 shows spending has not fallen below 36 per cent of GDP since 1948.

8 http://services.parliament.uk/bills/2009-10/fiscalresponsibility.html

9 http://www.publications.parliament.uk/pa/cm200910/cmhansrd/cm100105/debtext/100105-0012.htm

10 http://web.stanford.edu/~rabushka accessed 1 September 2014

11 Quoted at http://www.taxresearch.org.uk/Blog/ 2011/10/25/it-is-possible-to-have-a-flat-tax-or-to-have-democracy-but-not-both accessed 1 September 2014

12 Governor of the Bank of England Mark Carney suggested at the TUC Congress on 9 September 2014 that on average incomes had declined by 10 per cent in the UK since 2009.

13 http://www.bankofengland.co.uk/publications/ Documents/quarterlybulletin/2014/qb14q102.pdf page 21 accessed 26 August 2014

14 Ibid., page 14

15 Ibid., page 15

16 From *David Copperfield* by Charles Dickens: '[Mr Micawber] solemnly conjured me, I remember, to take warning by his fate; and to observe that if a man had twenty pounds a year for his income, and spent nineteen pounds nineteen shillings and sixpence, he would be happy, but that if he spent twenty pounds one [shilling] he would be miserable.' http://www.bartleby.com/380/prose/553. html

17 http://www.bankofengland.co.uk/about/pages/history/ default.aspx#2

18 Current household savings ratio at the time of writing is about 6 per cent of income, which is well above the rate from 1997 to 2008 on average: http://www.tradingeco-nomics.com/united-kingdom/personal-savings

19 http://www.theguardian.com/business/2015/feb/26/uk-business-investment-falls-at-fastest-rate-since-financial-crisis

20 http://www.ft.com/cms/s/2/1e1b9952-794f-11e3-91ac-

00144feabdc0.html#axzz3d6hyf79D

21 http://www.theguardian.com/business/2015/feb/06/uk-trade-deficit-widens-four-year-high

22 http://www.tradingeconomics.com/united-kingdom/personal-savings accessed 27 August 2014

23 http://www.ons.gov.uk/ons/rel/elmr/an-examination-of-falling-real-wages/2010-to-2013 art-an-examination-of-falling-real-wages.html accessed 27 August 2014

24 http://budgetresponsibility.org.uk/economic-fiscal-outlook-march-2014/ accessed 28 August 2014

25 http://cdn.budgetresponsibility.independent.gov.uk/March2015 EFO_18-03-webv1.pdf page 73 accessed 16 June 2015

26 http://cdn.budgetresponsibility.independent.gov.uk/March2015EFO_18-03-webv1.pdf page 55

27 http://www.tradingeconomics.com/united-kingdom/balance-of-trade

28 http://www.telegraph.co.uk/finance/budget/11465497/Budget-2015-There-are-two-versions-of-George-Osborne-and-the-radical-one-must-prevail.html accessed 16 June 2015

29 http://www.taxresearch.org.uk/Documents/Intheshade.pdf accessed 1 September 2014

30 Ibid.

31 http://www.taxresearch.org.uk/Documents/PCS TaxGap2014Full.pdf accessed 16 June 2015

32 https://www.gov.uk/government/uploads/system/uploads/attachment_data/file/345370/140819_Tackling_offshore_tax_evasion_-_A_new_criminal_offence.pdf

33 Scott Dyreng, Jeffrey L. Hoopes and Jaron H. Wilde, *Public Pressure and Corporate Tax Behavior* (July 29,

2014). Available at SSRN: http://ssrn.com/abstract=2474346

34 http://www.iea.org.uk/publications/research/the-benefits-of-tax-competition page 81

Chapter 5: Tax and choice

1 http://www.sbs.ox.ac.uk/ideas-impact/tax/about/funding

2 http://www.ifs.org.uk/publications/mirrleesreview

3 http://www.ifs.org.uk/uploads/mirrleesreview/dimensions/prelims.pdf

4 http://www.ft.com/cms/s/0/cac9ebe8-3d5c-11e2-b8b2-00144feabdc0.html#axzz3ELF6IAdg

5 https://www.sbs.ox.ac.uk/sites/default/files/Business_Taxation/Docs/Publications/Reports/TaxEvasionReportDFIDFINAL1906.pdf

6 See http://www.publications.parliament.uk/pa/cm201213/cmselect/cmtreasy/124/12405.htm

7 Partington v. Attorney-General (1869), L.R. 4 E. & I. App. 100, per Lord Cairns at page 122

8 http://www.hmrc.gov.uk/avoidance/gaar.htm

9 https://www.gov.uk/government/organisations/hmrevenue-customs/groups/hmrc-board

10 http://www.internationaltaxreview.com/Article/3201047/KPMG-Treasury-secondee-behind-UK-patent-box-hits-back-at-PAC-criticisms.html

11 http://www.publications.parliament.uk/pa/ld201415/ldhansrd/text/140716-0002.htm#1407172000119

12 http://www.standard.co.uk/comment/simon-jenkins-if-the-scots-can-get-taxraising-powers-so-should-london-9720747.html

13 http://www.thebureauinvestigates.com/2012/07/10/how-big-four-get-inside-track-by-loaning-staff-to-government

14 http://visar.csustan.edu/aaba/ProposedAccstd.pdf. I first created country-by-country reporting in 2003.

15 http://www.oecd-ilibrary.org/taxation/guidance-on-transfer-pricing-documentation-and-country-by-country-reporting_9789264219236-en

16 http://www.taxresearch.org.uk/Documents/CRDivCBCR2015.pdf

17 http://uncounted.org/2015/06/15/the-politics-of-country-by-country-reporting

Chapter 6: The underpinnings of a good tax system

1 Adam Smith, *The Wealth of Nations*, 1776, Book V, Chapter II, Part II. Extract downloaded from http://www.bibliomania.com/2/1/65/112/frameset.html 4 December 2006

2 It should be noted that these four terms are also the titles of what are called the Quaker Testimonies. I am a Quaker, but as far as I know, also the only one to ever interpret them in the way I do here. For more on the Quaker Testimonies see http://www.quaker.org.uk/testimonies

3 http://www.adamsmith.org/sites/default/files/images/stories/tax-competition.pdf

4 See, for example, http://www.adamsmith.org/research/think-pieces/save-the-tax-havens-we-need-them by the director of the Adam Smith Institute

5 The OECD is dedicated to ending it. See http://www.oecd.org/ctp/beps.htm

6 http://www.icij.org/project/luxembourg-leaks

7 http://www.financialsecrecyindex.com/PDF/SecrecyWorld.pdf

8 http://www.sussex.ac.uk/spru/people/lists/person/111262

9 http://classonline.org.uk/docs/2013_Policy_Paper_-_ Richard_Murphy__Howard_Reed_%28Social_State_-_ Idleness.pdf. The chart is based on data from the Office for National Statistics, 'The Effects of Taxes and Benefits on Household Income 2010–11', 2012; the methodology used to produce the results is an updated version of D. Byrne and S. Ruane, 'The UK Tax Burden: Can Labour be called the "party of fairness"?', 2008, Compass Thinkpiece.

10 https://www.atkearney.com/financial-institutions/ featured-article/-/asset_publisher/j8IucAqMqEhB/ content/the-shadow-economy-in-europe-2013/10192

11 http://www.americansfortaxfairness.org/files/ TheWalmartWeb-June-2015-FINAL.pdf

12 http://visar.csustan.edu/aaba/ProposedAccstd.pdf

13 http://www.oecd.org/tax/guidance-on-transfer-pricing- documentation-and-country-by-country-reporting- 9789264219236-en.htm

14 http://webarchive.nationalarchives.gov.uk/+/http://www. hmrc.gov.uk/history/taxhis1.htm accessed 26 November 2014

15 http://services.parliament.uk/bills/2012-13/generalanti taxavoidanceprinciple.html accessed 27 November 2014

Chapter 7: The policy decisions tax must impact

1 Male life expectancy at birth in 1945 was just 62.7 years, with women expecting 67.9 years of life. http://www.ons. gov.uk/ons/rel/social-trends-rd/social-trends/social- trends-41/health-data.xls. Those reaching age 65 did better, of course, expecting to live 13.2 years on average, a figure that has now increased to over 19 years.

2 http://www.ft.com/cms/s/2/b345d172-e1cd-11e4-bb7f-

00144feab7de.html#axzz3eQrJTr9K

3 https://www.gov.uk/government/uploads/system/uploads/
   attachment_data/file/407258/PEN6__2001-02_
   to_2013-14___for_publication.pdf

Chapter 8: The ideal tax system

1 http://brazilcham.com/articles/brazil-senate-rejects-
   renewal-of-cpmf-tax

2 http://classonline.org.uk/docs/2013_Policy_Paper_-_
   Richard_Murphy__Howard_Reed_(Social_State_-_
   Idleness.pdf page 27

3 http://classonline.org.uk/docs/2013_Policy_Paper_-_
   Richard_Murphy__Howard_Reed_(Social_State_-_
   Idleness.pdf

4 http://blogs.channel4.com/factcheck/factcheck-qa-
   benefit-fraud-perspective/15796

5 http://www.taxresearch.org.uk/Documents/
   PCSTaxGap2014Full.pdf

6 https://arctheunion.wordpress.com/2013/09/09/closing-
   the-tax-gap-delivering-for-the-nation

7 I should declare an interest: I have worked with PCS, the
   union for lower-grade HMRC staff.

8 https://www.gov.uk/government/organisations/hm-
   revenue-customs/groups/hmrc-board

9 http://www.parliament.uk/business/committees/
   committees-a-z/commons-select/public-accounts-
   committee/news   report-hmrc-progress-improving-
   preventing-tax-avoidance

10 http://www.parliament.uk/business/committees/commit-
   tees-a-z/commons-select/public-accounts-committee/
   news/hmrc-tax-disputes-report

11 http://www.theguardian.com/news/2015/feb/11/hmrc-

lenient-settlement-route-hsbc-suisse-clients

Chapter 9: As the Chancellor might put it

1 http://www.searchingfinance.com/products/soon-to-
   be-published/the-courageous-state-rethinking-economics-
   society-and-the-role-of-government.html
2 http://cdn.budgetresponsibility.independent.gov.uk/July-
   2015-EFO-234224.pdf
3 http://ec.europa.eu/eurostat/tgm/refreshTableAction.do?
   tab=table&plugin=1&pcode=tipspd20&language=en

Index

Bank of England (*cont.*)
  ownership and control of
    53–4+n, 57–60, 247–8
  on savings and investment
    56+n, 273–4
bank transactions, proposed
  tax on 221–3, 224, 229,
  275–6, 280, 281
  see also financial
    transactions tax
bankers 80, 119–20, 257
banking crisis and crash
  (2008) 91, 93, 225
banks and banking 56–7,
  58, 206, 214, 221, 247
  and money creation 55–6,
    247, 253
base rate (bank rate) 60n, 67
bedroom tax 279
Belgium 35–6
beliefs 44–5, 53n, 62
benefits systems 226–8
  see also welfare benefits
Bermuda 146, 160
Bible, references to taxation
  in 15, 16, 17
Boston Tea Party 24, 75
Brazil 222–3
Budget Responsibility, Office
  for 243
Buffett, Warren 266
Buiter, Willem 91
burden of proof 231, 257,
  265
burglary 40–1, 50

businesses
  assets 217
  investment by 104, 109,
    235
  and tax on transactions
    224
  see also companies
Butler, Eamonn 83

Cairns, Lord 130–1
Cameron, David 96
capital gains 215, 217,
  266–8
capital gains tax 32, 34, 85,
  266–8, 269, 271
capping
  council tax 33, 269–70
  flat taxes and 87–90, 91–3
carbon usage 224, 225, 276
Carney, Mark 97n
Carville, James 25
case law 131
Cayman Islands 146
Center for Freedom and
  Prosperity 158
central banks 57, 62
  see also Bank of England
certainty 153–4
charities 48
Charter of Liberties 18, 24
child credits 279
children 228
CIA Factbook 39
citizen's income 227–30
City of London 20, 221